"Hello, Sucker!"

Texas Guinan as The Spitfire *(Texas Guinan Productions-Merit Film Company, 1922).*

"Hello, Sucker!"
The Story of
Texas Guinan

By

GLENN SHIRLEY

EAKIN PRESS ★ AUSTIN, TEXAS

Library of Congress Cataloging-in-Publication Data

Shirley, Glenn.
    "Hello, sucker!"

Bibliography: p.
    1. Guinan, Texas. 2. Entertainers — United States — Biography. I. Title.
PN2287.G75S5   1989   792'.028'0924   [B]   88-33530
ISBN 0-89015-690-5

Contents

Preface

Who was "Texas" Guinan?

She is best remembered as the firebrand hostess of Broadway's high revel during the Prohibition era, who turned New York's nightlife into what she was fond of calling "an essential and basic industry." In the heyday of her success she is said to have banked $700,000 in one ten-month period. She enriched the nation's idiom with a cascade of wisecracks and eccentric salutations, such as "hello, sucker!" and "big-butter-and-egg man," and despite the doubtful artistic talents of her female performers, insisted that her patrons "give the little girl a great big hand."

From the mid-1920s into the early 1930s, she struggled constantly with local and federal authorities, censorship boards, and even foreign governments to stay out of jail, keep her establishments open, and put her traveling revues on the road. She even spurred the government's purchase of padlocks — all of which far overshadowed her earlier vaudeville career and starring roles in scores of silent westerns as "the female William S. Hart of the screen."

"My real name," she said in one interview with the New York press in 1929, "is Mary Louise Cecilia Guinan, but I've nearly forgotten that they christened me that. I was born on a ranch near Waco, Texas, so many years ago that it's nobody's business." New York police blotters show the year of birth as 1889. One motion picture studio directory and trade annual says 1891. Exercising a woman's prerogative, she stated her age as considerably less than what it actually was.

She provided few details of her childhood, and for some reason journalists did not pursue the matter. Perhaps her growing-up period seemed insignificant in light of her Prohibition-era fame and her view of Broadway through a keyhole.

CHAPTER 1

"Mamie" Becomes "Texas"

Contrary to the romantic nonsense that some journalists attributed to the birth of Mary Louise Cecilia Guinan, the most that can be said of the occasion is that she came kicking and squalling into the world at Waco, Texas, on January 12, 1884, and was baptized next day at the Church of the Assumption of St. Mary. Her parents, Michael and Bessie (Duffy) Guinan, were Irish immigrants who had arrived in the area two years previously.

Michael Guinan, a hardy lad, had sailed from Dublin to make his fortune in America, stopping first in Denver, Colorado, where he learned the wholesale grocery business and became part owner and manager of a company. Bessie Duffy had also sailed from her native Dublin, stopping by chance in Denver. The two met, romanced, and wed. Shortly afterwards, Michael disposed of his grocery interests and the couple settled on a small ranch near Waco to raise horses, cattle, and four children. Their brood, besides the exuberant Mary Louise Cecilia, consisted of two sons, William (Willie) and Thomas (Tommy), and a second daughter, the youngest child, Pearl.

Mary Louise Cecilia's name was shortened for a brief period to "Mamie." During her early years she managed to maintain a ladylike behavior, attended parochial school at Loretta Convent, and sang regularly in the church choir. Her parents hoped for a musical career. But developments of drama and music were slow in coming to that section of Texas, and Mamie was more inclined to hoyden-ish pranks, such as climbing to the church steeple and removing the bell clapper.

Many of her actions were the outgrowth of an unusual interest in the region's history. Waco, seat of McLennan County, stood near the confluence of the Bosque and Brazos rivers on the location of a once famous spring that supplied water to an ancient village of the Waco Indians, a Wichita tribe closely related to the Tawakoni. The first white settlement on the site was a Ranger outpost, Fort Fisher, established in 1837 to suppress the Waco, who were on the warpath with other tribes. The Waco made peace with the Repub-lic of Texas in 1843 and were finally expelled with other Wichita to Indian Territory (now Oklahoma).

Choice names in Mamie's lexicon were George Barnard, who opened a trading post on Tehaucana Creek in 1844; Jesse Sutton, who erected a log blacksmith shop in 1846; Shapley Prince Ross, company commander in a Ranger battalion mustered for the pro-tection of the frontier in 1847, who built the first hotel, became the first postmaster, served as Indian agent (1855–1858), and died at Waco in 1889; George B. Erath, a native Austrian, who came to Texas in 1832 to work as a surveyor at Tenoxtitlan, fought at San Jacinto, was a member of the first Texas legislature in 1846, laid out the town of Waco in 1849, and made it his home until his death in 1891; and Neil McLennan, for whom the county was named when it was organized in 1850. McLennan, a native of Scotland, had fought with the Rangers during the Indian uprisings of the 1830s, returned to the area to plant crops and build a house on the South Bosque River, and lived there until his death in 1867.

Waco's commerce, dependent largely upon the rich planta-tions of the Brazos Valley, suffered severely during the Civil War. It recovered rapidly with the beginning of the cattle business on the Chisholm Trail. In 1870 a suspension bridge, then the longest in the world, was completed across the Brazos at Waco, resulting in a stream of commerce that earned for the town the title "Hub City."

By 1890 McLennan County had 166 miles of railroad. The Waco Tap was built to Bremond in 1871 and extended to Ross in 1873. The Gulf, Colorado and Santa Fe crossed the county in 1881; the Missouri, Kansas and Texas reached Waco from the north that same year; the Waco, Beaumont, Trinity and Sabine built westward from Waco to Gatesville in 1882; and Waco became the northern terminus of the San Antonio and Aransas Pass railroad in 1889. The county had ten banks, several newspapers, and a dozen flour, woolen, and cotton-seed mills and cotton and canning factories. Its population had increased to 60,000. Some 600 farms were producing 21,000 bales of cotton annually, while hog, sheep, cattle, and horse ranching rated second in importance — the industry which had brought Michael Guinan to Texas. The county was also considered of special political importance, having furnished the state two governors, Richard Coke and Lawrence Sullivan Ross.

Mamie Guinan had every opportunity for a formal education. Waco had a number of excellent institutions of higher learning, including the Waco Female College, chartered in 1860, and Waco University, which absorbed the Waco Classical School in 1861, combined with Baylor at Independence in 1886, and rechartered as Baylor University on the Waco campus in 1887. The academic standards of these schools earned the city another name, "Athens of Texas."

But it was the early cattle drives, Indian battles, and other exploits of McLennan County's pioneers that held Mamie's fascination. On her father's ranch she learned to ride, rope, and tame unruly broncs. She was a frequent visitor at the local shooting gallery next to the Missouri, Kansas and Texas railroad depot, and was soon hitting targets with a six-shooter from the back of her running mount. At age fourteen she made an impromptu appearance at a frontier days celebration, where her equestrian and roping skills delighted an audience of thousands and won her the sobriquet "Texas."

All of which displeased her parents.

That same year Marshall Field of Chicago offered a singing scholarship to the American Conservatory of Music. This merchant king, who started life as a farm boy in Conway, Massachusetts, and became the nation's "Model Millionaire," had long been the idol of Michael Guinan.

Field had mastered the dry goods business as a clerk in a Pittsfield, Massachusetts, store at age seventeen. In 1856 he entered the mercantile house of Cooley, Wadsworth and Company at Chicago, where he rendered such valuable service that he was admitted to partnership. In 1860 the firm name was changed to Cooley, Farwell and Company, and later to Farwell, Field and Company. On dissolution of this partnership the firm of Field, Palmer and Leiter was formed in 1865, and on the retirement of Potter Palmer, two years later, the firm became Field, Leiter and Company. In 1881 Field purchased the Leiter interest and continued the firm under the name Marshall Field and Company. It was now a $60 million business that paid profits of approximately $10 million annually.

He and his family resided in a palace on Prairie Avenue. His trade structures covered a white "marble block" on State Street and a red "granite block" in the wholesale district, and he owned many other buildings in which factories of all kinds were making goods for the Chicago houses and large stores in New York, England, France, and Germany, looked after by trusted lieutenants. In addition, he owned bonds and stocks in United States Steel, of which he was a director and leading spirit, and in streetcar, railway, and other companies which owned the principal utilities of Chicago.

Great as Field's mercantile and corporate interests were, they had become secondary to his philanthropy. He had donated $450,000 in land and money to the University of Chicago, the institution to which John D. Rockefeller had given millions. With a gift of one million dollars he had founded the Field Columbian Museum for the preservation of rare specimens in ethnological and natural history exhibits at the Columbian Exposition of 1893 and, at a cost of $200,000, had given and endowed a public library to his native town of Conway.

When the Guinans learned of the Field singing scholarship, they hied their plucky, blue-eyed offspring away to the Windy City. Mamie won the scholarship, and for the next two years she studied diligently in the conservatory and in the School of Dramatic Arts. She then returned home and graduated from the classy Hollins School for Girls.

In 1902 she traveled with a Waco stock company, a group that proved unsuccessful. The wide-open spaces called again, and she resorted to her former avenues of endeavor, touring several western states and territories as an itinerant performer in rodeos (then called "roundups").

While riding for a Wild West circus in Colorado, she met and married a roving newspaper artist, John J. Moynahan. The marriage certificate in the Bureau of Records at Denver, dated December 2, 1904, gives her name as "Marie" Guinan.

Little is known of this union, except that it was of short duration. Moynahan became a newspaper executive in Boston, and by 1906, Texas was in New York, seeking a place in the legitimate theater and vaudeville. She was saddened that year by news of the death of her benefactor, Marshall Field.

Following an eight-day bout with pneumonia contracted while in New York on business, Field died at the Hollard House on January 16 with members of his family in constant attendance at his bedside. The body was taken next day by special train over the New York Central-Hudson River-Lake Shore System to Chicago, where funeral services were held January 19 at the Field palace on Prairie Avenue and at the First Presbyterian Church.

Texas did not attend the services. She was immersed in the dizzying pace of life in New York.

CHAPTER 2

From Gibson Girl to
The Passing Show

Though acclimated to big city life by her sojourns in Denver and
Chicago, Texas Guinan was amazed by the turn-of-the-century
vastness of New York City.

Beginning at the lower end of Manhattan Island, the city
spread over 327 square miles north and east on the shores of the
Hudson and North rivers, Long Island Sound, and the Atlantic.
The borough of Manhattan, laid out in rectangular avenues and
streets above Fourteenth, was the business center, with the chief re-
tail business streets — Broadway, Sixth Avenue, and the Bowery —
running north and northwest for miles. Fourteenth, Twenty-third,
and Forty-second streets ran across the island east and west. The
financial interests of the city and nation were centered on Wall and
Broad streets east of Broadway, near the southern end of the island.
Fifth and Madison avenues, for many years the finest residential
streets, were giving way to Riverside and West End avenues, overlooking the Hudson and set with elegant mansions. The city's population of 3,435,202 in the census of 1900 had increased in 1906 to
four million, and it was the most remarkable collection of people
and the most various in race and religion ever gathered in such
numbers in the history of mankind.

America moved into the new century ravenous for entertainment, and the show business responded in kind. Spectacular circuses and Wild West shows traveled from city to city in special trains with as many as ninety cars. Hundreds of "medicine show" enterprises touted remedies, cures, and health formulas in almost every village and hamlet, and used some form of showmanship or ballyhoo to attract attention and overcome customer resistance. Touring stock companies carried drama of a new, earthy texture to theaters and opera houses of the provinces. The legend on bills, "Direct from Broadway, Original New York Cast," announced the coming of another New York success. Many a good play that failed in the metropolis found unbounded acceptance on the road.

The favorite entertainment for the average person was vaudeville. Its patter and knockabout acrobatics delighted audiences, but reaction was mixed regarding the usual fare of ventriloquists, jugglers, singers, animal acts, and such standard gags as "I sent my wife to the Thousand Islands for a vacation — a week on each island" or "You can drive a horse to drink but a pencil must be lead." Some acts were so utterly bad that the players performed behind a net to protect themselves from overripe fruits and vegetables, and were relegated to deserved obscurity.

Tin Pan Alley thrived as never before. Sheet music and pianola rolls sold by the carload, and "hit" songs earned their composers and lyricists royalties as high as $50,000. Censored tunes like "Her Name Was Mary Wood But Mary Wouldn't," "Angle Worm Wiggle," and "I Love My Wife But Oh, You Kid" were banned in many cities. Barbershop quartets revered "Sweet Adeline," "Down By the Old Mill Stream" and "Girl of My Dreams." The decade gave birth to the first popular cowboy songs, "Cheyenne" and "San Antonio," and scores of such still standard favorites as "In My Merry Oldsmobile," "After the Ball," "My Gal Sal," "Wait Until the Sun Shines, Nellie," "Bicycle Built For Two," "Take Me Out to the Ball Game," and "What You Goin' to Do When the Rent Comes 'Round?"

Texas Guinan wondered too. She found the going in New York much rougher than she expected. She lived in a two-dollar-a-week hotel on Washington Square and haunted the offices of theater casting agents, without finding work.

One day, when down to her last shekel, she spotted a Great Arrow automobile shining in a display window. America had only 8,000 cars at the turn of the century. Though everyone was fascinated with the "horseless carriage" and flocked to auto shows, they generally considered it a costly contraption that "balked, trembled and clattered, spat oil, fire, smell and smoke." Only those with fat wallets were buyers. Plutocrats on their way to spas and shore resorts aroused widespread resentment of the countryman by running down livestock and driving off as fast as possible. In the cities, these drivers angered pedestrians by racing through the streets at more than ten miles per hour, and often evaded bicycle-mounted police. In 1906, Woodrow Wilson, then president of Princeton, anxiously labeled the motorist "a picture of arrogance of wealth, with all its independence and carelessness."

But the backlash was changing. Within a couple of years the homely creation of a self-taught engineer named Henry Ford would hit the nation's byways as "The Universal Car." Meanwhile, Oldsmobile, Locomobile, Packard, and other manufacturers stuck to the powerful product — new models incorporating more speed and greater elegance. The car of the decade, the Great Arrow, was so prestigious that whoever could afford it obviously did not have to ask the price ($4,500 up), since that information was snobbishly omitted in its advertising.

Texas Guinan had visions of one day being chauffeured in such opulence, of enjoying the new and exciting life on wheels. For the moment, she had to rely on one of her many talents. During her brief stay with newspaper artist Moynahan, she had learned something of the rudiments of illustrating. She invested her last pennies in some paper and pencils and hastily sketched the flashy car, then sold her finished drawing to an advertising agency for $500.

In June of 1905, Joe C., Zack T., and George L. Miller, sons of George Washington Miller, who had founded the famed 101 Ranch, had staged a roundup for the National Editorial Association holding its convention in Oklahoma. The spectacular displays of riding, roping, and bulldogging, as well as an attack on a wagon train by two hundred Indians, a personal appearance by the old Apache chief Geronimo, and a buffalo hunt in which buffalo were killed to feed some 60,000 guests, were publicized throughout the land. In 1907 the Millers were invited to give an arena display of their features at the Jamestown Exposition at Norfolk, Virginia. This show was such a triumph that the Millers hurried back to Oklahoma, recruited another show from their abundant resources, and took it to Brighton Beach, New York, where it broke metropolitan records for six weeks. Edward Arlington, a veteran of the Barnum and Bailey circus and general agent for the Pawnee Bill Wild West Show, persuaded them to go on the road permanently.

Texas Guinan had declined the Millers' invitation to perform at Jamestown, but she might have joined their second show at Brighton Beach had not an agent obtained a place for her in a chorus. With her foot finally in the door for a possible theater career, which she really wanted, she remained in New York.

Texas continued to make the rounds of agents and eventually was cast in a play titled *The Snow Man*. In 1908 she was reported doing very well along the vaudeville circuits, having been featured in an act called "The Gibson Girl."

As the automobile industry had struggled into high gear, so had American women. Charles Dana Gibson's pen-and-ink conceptions of the ideal girl — "divinely tall, brows like Juno, lovely heads poised on throats Aphrodite might envy, superbly dressed, artful but never truly wicked" — appeared in the old comic weekly, *Life*, and overnight became the idol and model for a generation. Gibson, who used his cartoons and serialized picture stories to poke fun at society, was astonished by the adulation. He kindly granted permission to use his girls on everything from china plates to bedroom pillows. Women looked upon his girls as style-setters. As one contemporary observed, "You can tell when a girl is taking the Gibson Cure by the way she fixes her hair." Men were just as smitten. They imitated the handsome swains who always attended the girls in Gibson's drawings, shaved their mustaches, padded the shoulders of their jackets, and decorated their bachelor apartments with Gibson girl wallpaper.

Texas Guinan, in her "Gibson Girl" act, displayed her five-foot-six, leggy, buxom figure and dispensed a song or two. In 1909 she inaugurated a new version, suspended in a basket above the heads of the audience and rhapsodizing such noble sentiments as "Pansies Bring Thoughts of You."

Always desirous of improving her performances, she studied vaudeville's leading single women stars, like Lillian Russell, Mae West, and Eva Tanguay.

Miss Tanguay, very beautiful and a fine singer with a terrific personality, represented the true spirit of vaudeville. She came up the hard way, starting in the chorus, clowning and showing her legs. When the Salome craze hit New York in 1908, and the single women, one after another, started doing the dance, Eva Tanguay "busted things wide open" by discarding all seven veils. In 1909 she was in the *Ziegfeld Follies,* her name billed as big as the show. She electrified audiences with songs written specially for her — "Egotistical Eva," "Give an Imitation of Eva," "I Can't Help It," "Whistle and Help Me Along" — and her most widely acclaimed hit, "I Don't Care." In 1910 her weekly salary was $2,500 — the highest paid at the time to a lone performer. When her booking office refused to up the ante, she took her own show on the road and earned twice what she had asked. She had something to deliver, and was the most imitated woman of the so-called Golden Dozen.

At the Model Theater in Philadelphia, brassy and bosomy Mae West was making the public eye blink singing "Rag Rag Rag," accompanied by some lethargic but meaningful body gestures while seated in a chair. One ad plugging her act called it "a muscle dance in a sitting position — it is all in the way she does it, and her way is all her own." When she appeared with a show in New Haven, the Yale undergraduates all but tore the house down. The show biz tabloid, *Variety,* suggested that "Miss West be coached to deliver the full value of her personality." She did just that later at the American Roof by wearing a trick dress with a strap that broke easily, and calmly insisted to the complaining manager that she couldn't help it if the garment was defective. Before she opened on Broadway with a play she had written, *Sex,* nobody had dared ever print the word in public. But there it was on a theater marquee. The play was a smash at an unheard of $10 a seat. It also landed Mae West in jail for eight days at Welfare Island, where she won national fame with her demands, finally granted, that jailers provide her with silk underwear.

West was an institution when she made her film debut in Hollywood in 1932, bringing Paramount Studios out of the red and keeping the reformers and censors tearing their hair. "Virtue has its own reward, but has no sale at the box office," she said, then laid her curves on the couch and purred in her tantalizing drawl: "Come up and see me sometime."

Texas incorporated some of Miss Tanguay's routines, without imitating, and she respected Mae West's wit and philosophy. But her popular favorite was Lillian Russell.

A comic opera singer from Iowa, Miss Russell had appeared in *Pinafore* under the direction of E. E. Rice in 1879 and later at Tony

Pastor's Fourteenth Street Theater, in New York. She soon became the star in the McCaull Opera Company, playing leading parts in *Snake Charmer, Olivette, Patience,* and *The Sorcerer,* and sang in London in 1883. She returned to New York in 1885 and sang at the Casino in various roles and at Webber and Fields music hall until she condescended to step down to vaudeville — as did many Metropolitan Opera stars — in 1905. She retained her hold as a top box-office attraction, and sparked an otherwise poor 1909 season by opening in *The Widow's Night.*

Texas had the opportunity to meet Miss Russell several times. She so impressed this lady of the hour-glass figure that she became a protegé, and won increasingly better roles in such musical comedy favorites as *Miss Bob White, The Hoyden,* and *The Gay Musician.*

While touring with *The Gay Musician,* she accidentally shot herself in the side and was rushed to a hospital. Though her injuries were serious, she quickly recovered and declared to reporters: "Nothing — not even a bullet — can stop Texas Guinan!"

Moving up in the theatrical world, she soon was on stage in *The Kissing Girl.* A blue-nosed critic named Julian Johnson panned her performance unmercifully. Shortly thereafter, when they met by chance at a luncheon, it was loathing at first sight. But something else happened. Texas may have taught her critic what kissing was all about, because a year later they were wed.

Texas continued to do well in vaudeville after the close of the century's first decade, appearing on stage in *Hop 'O My Thumb* with DeWolf Hopper, popular star of numerous shows and of "Casey at the Bat" fame.

Musical comedy was big in 1912. Joe Weber and Lew Fields reunited to open their new Lew Fields Music Hall on 44th Street with a cast of greats including Marie Dressler and Bessie Clayton. Will Rogers, Oklahoma's "ropin' topical commentator," had graduated from the New York Stars Burlesque Company and was featured with Blanche Ring in his first Broadway show, *Wall Street Gal.* The sixth *Ziegfeld Follies* was *the* box-office attraction with the song lyrics of Gene Buck, who later produced many *Follies* editions and more than a score of Ziegfeld's *Midnight Frolics.* The Shubert Brothers offered the first *Passing Show* revue in New York's Winter Garden, starring Willie and Eugene Howard with Trixie Friganza and Charlotte Greenwood. In the *Passing Show* of 1913, Texas Guinan was one of the stars.

In conjunction with her *Passing Show* performance, Texas lent her name to a weight-loss promoter, who ran ads in *Variety* and elsewhere offering a "Marvelous New Treatment for Fat Folks." A picture of Guinan in dazzling costume was captioned: "God's Masterpiece and the Most Fascinating Actress in America." Later in the year, when the post office department prosecuted the promoter, Texas testified: "I was made a star of the *Passing Show* on account of my glorious figure . . . and mind you, I was doomed to oblivion just a short time before when I tipped the scales at 204 pounds . . ." Texas weighed at most only 136 pounds in her life.

CHAPTER 3

Call of the Silver Screen

Unlike Mae West's eight-day stint at Welfare Island in later years, publicity in the weight-loss case damaged Texas Guinan's climb to stardom. However, she was not discouraged. She remained in vaudeville, her hopes no longer centered on becoming a Tanguay or Russell but on getting into a rapidly developing industry called "moving pictures."

In 1893 Thomas A. Edison had completed his first studio for the production of Kinestoscope films to supply the growing number of peepshows, and a year later constructed his famous Black Maria Studio at his plant in West Orange, New Jersey. There he produced hundreds of "Circle E" Vitascope subjects that were intermingled with theater variety bills. In Chicago, Col. William Nicholas Selig's Polyscope Company, founded in 1896, was grinding out a dozen "Diamond S" films a week; the George Kleine Optical Company, a lantern slide operation at its outset, had developed into moving picture distribution; and George K. Spoor was competitively supplying films for both his vaudeville circuit showings and clamoring showmen. In Pennsylvania, Sigmund Lubin, another optician and early entrant in the industry with his Lubin Manufacturing Company, made subject pictures under the trademark of the Liberty Bell. He later owned a string of theaters in Philadelphia.

In 1903 Edwin Stratton Porter, a former U.S. Navy mechanic and electrician who had collaborated with Edison in developing the moving picture camera, prevailed on the Delaware, Lackawanna and Western railroad to loan him a special train and the use of its line near Dover, New Jersey, to film a ten-minute western epic called *The Great Train Robbery*. Western outlaws and railroad holdups were of topical interest, badmen like the Daltons, Youngers and James Boys having been glamorized in dime novels, along with their nemesis, the "cowboy" detective. Porter's movie was adapted from Scott Marble's *The Great Train Robbery*, performed at New York's Bowery Theater several years previously.

The Great Train Robbery created a sensation. It played to packed houses on its first runs at Huber's Museum, the Eden Musee, and at Hammerstein's. And it set a style for picture drama that told a story in several scenes. Narrative film art was born.

The Great Train Robbery also launched the western movie career of Gilbert M. "Max" Anderson (born Aronson). Struck by the scarcity of pictures available to George K. Spoor's National Film Renting Company, Anderson went to Chicago, where he and Spoor launched the Essanay Film Company (derived from their last initials, "S" and "A"). In 1908 they established a studio at Niles, California, on the San Francisco Bay. An estimated 374 comedies and "Broncho Billy" Anderson westerns rolled from its cameras during the next seven years.

Meanwhile, thousands of unused storerooms and small theaters across the country were converted into exhibition halls, called "nickel parlors," "nickelets," or "nickelodeons," where fifty to 300 people could see twelve to eighteen shows daily at five cents, and the number increased.

So did the number of film-producing companies. The East Coast (primarily New York City and northern New Jersey) became the capital of the new industry and remained its center until the end of the nickelodeon era and migration to the West Coast displaced it with Hollywood.

In 1906 the Vitagraph Company of America opened a studio on Long Island and, in 1911, one in California. Vitagraph, which used the letter "V" trademark surmounted by an eagle with spread wings, specialized in the works of Shakespeare and parlor comedies, and would produce thousands of other interesting films before it was sold to Warner Brothers in 1925.

In 1907 the Midwest distributor George Kleine formed an independent company in New York City, producing films under the sign of the blazing sun and the word "Kalem," inspired from the surname initials of Kleine and his partners, Samuel Long and Frank Marion (K, L, and M). The company also pioneered in world productions, sending troupes to Egypt and Israel as early as 1911, and maintained a studio in Ireland.

In 1909 the New York Motion Picture Company, importing agent for foreign films in New York City, formed its own production firm under the "Bison" trademark derived from the animal portrait on the contemporary $10 currency note. The first Bison films were made in New Jersey, and finally at a studio established in Edendale, California, for making westerns. In 1911 Bison made a deal with the Miller Brothers' 101 Ranch Wild West Show (in winter quarters at Venice, California), adopting the "101 Bison" trademark. The trademark was used almost exclusively for this branch operation until the Bison name was lost to Universal and its western output resumed by two newly formed companies, Broncho and Kay-Bee.

The American Mutoscope and Biograph Company had offices in New York City and a studio in California, where David Wark Griffith produced nearly 400 subjects for Biograph before he, Mack Sennett, and Thomas H. Ince began making the really great dramas that changed the industry from a peepshow affair. Griffith, Ince, and Sennett also served as production heads for Triangle Film Corporation, a combine of Reliance/Majestic, the New York Motion Picture Company, and Keystone, instituted in July 1915.

Scores of smaller independents instituted during this period survived only a few months or years before they folded or were combined with the big producers.

Edison built a new studio in Bronx Park, held onto his motion picture patents, and while licensing some companies, fought court battles to prevent independents from making films. In September 1908 he formed the Motion Pictures Company (referred to by his adversaries as a "trust"), which included Biograph, Kleine, Kalem, Lubin, Selig, Vitagraph, and others. In 1915 the Kleine-Edison Feature Films Service was organized to handle distribution for company members, leasing out an estimated 5,000 movie machines and providing some 2,000 reels a week.

Fierce competition came from the Independent Moving Pictures Company of New York, with Carl Laemmle as president, which made films under a shield design bearing the letters "IMP." The first IMP production was *Hiawatha,* released in October 1909. The following year King Baggot joined IMP, and soon became a popular star and film director. In 1912 Laemmle formed the Universal Film Manufacturing Company, merging IMP with the Universal group which included Powers, Champion, Republic, Nestor, and later Rex, Eclair, and Victor films.

Another big competitor was Famous Players Film Company, formed in 1912 by Adolph Zukor and Daniel Frohman under the slogan "Famous Players in Famous Plays." It was joined by Jesse L. Lasky in 1914 and adopted the new name Famous Players-Lasky. Oliver Morosco and Hobart Bosworth, with their independent units, also joined the company. Paramount Pictures Corporation served as the distributing outlet for all movies under the Famous Players-Lasky banner and later became the company name and one of the major Hollywood trademarks.

As movie theaters continued to blossom across the country, vaudeville managers and veteran show business magnates, who had referred to film as "the tape" and the "poor man's amusement," began to sit up and take notice. Touring road companies were crumbling in the face of this cheaper competition. Vaudeville shows often cost more to run than they were grossing, and were forced to add movies to their bills. There were rumors of new developments for color photography and a "talking-singing" picture machine recently brought over from England.

The public taste was for more sustained narrative — a larger and better story with action. Filmmakers began buying "ideas" from top magazine writers and novelists like Zona Gale, E. Phillips Oppenheim, and Mary Roberts Rinehart. Plot lines required longer features, shooting locations other than rooftops and studios under glass roofs or with artificial light, outdoor locales other than in New Jersey or New York across-the-Hudson, and performers who might both look and act a particular role. Blanche Ring, DeWolf Hopper, and other Broadway favorites signed to do their acts for the screen. It also attracted great theatrical figures like Maude Adams, Billie Burke, Fay Templeton, George Arliss, Douglas Fairbanks, and the Barrymores (John, Lionel, and Ethel). The film colony in Los Angeles organized a Photoplayers Club, and the "star" system came into being.

These developments finally strangled the Edison company, which due to its shortsightedness kept marketing one- and two-reelers produced on-the-spot.

By 1916 films had become a "high art." According to *Picture-Play Magazine,* they "occupied fifth place among the industries of the United States, being surpassed by railroads, the clothing industry, iron and steel, and oil. The automobile manufacturer is minor in importance."

Western pictures packed the movie houses and were ready money-makers for producers, much to the credit of Broncho Billy Anderson, Tom Mix (former 101 Ranch cowboy), and the former New York stage actor William S. Hart. Anderson's western series ran 366 consecutive weeks in many theaters. In 1913 he created a riot by appearing in New York streets and restaurants and was forced to flee from the ardent embraces of his admirers.

By 1916 Hart had starred in some thirty features produced successively by the New York Motion Picture Company, Triangle Film Corporation, and Kay-Bee, all under the supervision of Thomas H. Ince. Many were written in part and directed by Hart himself. Mix starred in nearly 200 films for Selig from 1909 to 1917, when he cast his lot with the Fox Film Corporation and became "King of the Cowboys."

Westerns were further enhanced by bringing to the screen the popular novels of Rex Beach, Bertha Muzzy Bower, John Fox, Jr., Owen Wister, Frank Hamilton Spearman, Zane Grey, and Peter B. Kyne.

Texas Guinan found the genre in harmony with both her background and talents. As she stated, in a 1929 interview, "I could twirl a lariat, rope a steer, ride — and shoot to beat any tobacco-chewin' cowpoke." Her "big chance" for the movies came in early 1917, when she was discovered by a scout for the Balboa Amusement Producing Company. Balboa, operated by the Horkheimer Brothers, distributed its products through Famous Players-Lasky and had its plant at Long Beach, California.

Guinan recalled: "We poor chorus girls (at the Winter Garden) were always looking for some new stunt whereby to distinguish ourselves, so when I asked the manager if I might ride a horse down the runway instead of merely dancing down, he said, 'All right, if you don't kill too many customers.' I'll admit most of them got under their seats when they saw me ride my snow-white charger thundering down the runway above their heads, all dressed up in black lace chaps and swinging a lariat . . . After the show the movie man signed me up (for) a two-reel western . . . and what a time I had!"

The movie, titled *The Wildcat,* was released May 3, 1917, a month after President Woodrow Wilson delivered his war message to Congress and Congress passed the war declaration against Germany.

How *The Wildcat* fared is not known. The nation was swept by sudden change, hysteria and confusion, plagued with rocketing prices and shortages. Box-office receipts fell badly as ticket money went to buy War Savings Stamps and Liberty Bonds and millions of young male theatergoers reported for close-order drill under the first draft act. Millions more became obsessed with war plant overtime.

One branch of the show business thrived — cabarets — which included hotels, cafes, saloons, and dives that sold liquor (though two-thirds of the American people were then living in Prohibition states), with entertainment as an added attraction. Entertainers also found a new outlet in the Liberty Theaters (forerunner of the USO camp shows of World War II) that were hastily constructed at army posts for servicemen.

By June, American troops and supplies were pouring into France in what seemed an endless stream. Gen. John J. Pershing, commander-in-chief of the American Expeditionary Force, sailed to London at once to assume his duties. On June 13 he was in Paris, where he maintained his headquarters for a time and then moved to Chaumont, south of Verdun, within easy reach of the sector of the front which he perceived to be the scene of the American army's operation.

Texas Guinan, as did many other show people, volunteered to entertain the troops in France. For her services below Verdun, she was awarded a Bronze Medal by French Field Marshal Joseph Jacques Joffre.

At the end of summer in 1917, Texas Guinan was back in New York. Vaudeville remained in uncertain straits; cabarets and Liberty Theaters held no future. Her laudable performance in *The Wildcat* (or perhaps it was her Bronze Medal) got a sympathetic ear at Harry Aitken's Triangle Film Corporation in Yonkers.

Triangle needed girls who could ride, shoot, and handle a lariat. However, few women who sought stardom in the man's world of westerns had risen to a position beyond providing love interest or support for the handsome male heroes. Aitken had doubted that fans would identify well with a female who could settle range wars, clean out a town's undesirables, and bring in desperados who had robbed the local bank.

Texas insisted. Her argument: Both daring men and women had conquered and settled the American West. Rodeos and Wild West shows gave equal status to the female; why not the cinematic version? In cowboy gear, with her mop of black hair, she could look menacing enough to scare off the villain even without using a six-shooter.

Since organizing Triangle as a combine of Reliance/Majestic, the New York Motion Picture Company, and Keystone in 1915, Aitken had been obsessed with signing up Broadway stars and turning them over to his production heads, Griffith, Ince, and Sennett. While performers like Marie Doro, Sir Beerbohm Tree, Elliott Dexter, and DeWolf Hopper impressed the theater-going citizenry of New York City, their names on film house marquees meant nothing to other Americans and usually kept audiences away. Aitken ignored that fact. He had incurred no difficulty in obtaining Wall Street financing to get Triangle on its way and was able to lease New York's Knickerbocker Theatre as the glittering showcase for its top productions. Film exhibitors across the nation were impressed by the advance publicity and promises of the corporation, and Aitken reveled in its handful of stars that became screen successes (Douglas Fairbanks, Gloria Swanson, Francis McDonald, Alma Rubens, Mae Busch, and William S. Hart). In fact, Hart's films, and the dashing comedic westerns of Fairbanks, kept many of Triangle's exhibitors out of the red.

Guinan's idea of an authentic lady gunslinger on the celluloid prairie intrigued Triangle directors. Aitken decided that the anomaly might work and signed her for a series of pictures.

The three producers who made up the corners of the "triangle" had separate studios in California. Griffith was on the old Majestic/Reliance lot in Hollywood, Ince operated "Inceville" in

Santa Ynez Canyon near Santa Monica, and Sennett operated his original "laugh factory" at Edendale. Though the expense of a single studio for Triangle was unnecessary, Aitken had constructed a "Glass Greenhouse" with stages along Washington Boulevard in Culver City so that the firm's productions might be "compactly grouped."

Texas was sent to Culver City. Her husband, Julian Johnson, became the scenario editor at the studio. In October and November 1917, she starred in three westerns: *Get-Away Kate, Fuel of Life,* and *The Stainless Barrier.* Her image of self-reliant womanhood — a cowgirl in chaps with six-shooter in hand who could meet the bullying masculine world on its own terms — caught fire and was well promoted. In 1918 she starred in three more melodramas: *The Gun Woman* (with Francis McDonald), *The Love Brokers* (with Alma Rubens), and *The Hellcat.*

Guinan became one of the big names at Triangle. She also was noted for her unique dressing room. Instead of a name plate, a map of Texas decorated her door. The door knocker was an orange parrot, and the interior was of orange wicker and black velvet. When not hard at work before the cameras, she lounged there in orange and black pajamas and served tea to her many friends. She and her husband often entertained young Gloria Swanson, then playing in Keystone comedies.

Had Texas been afforded the tutelage of Griffith, Ince, or Sennett, she might have achieved the fame of Fairbanks and Hart. However, Triangle chose to "cash in" on these name producers by employing a sizable number of directors to work under them. Under Griffith's supervision alone were several directors like Sidney Franklin, Raoul Walsh, Allan Dawn, and W. S. Van Dyke.

How Texas fared with one sub-director is exemplified in filming of *The Hellcat.*

"It was to be shot on location," she recalled in 1926, "in the Big Bear country of northwestern Canada." The plot involved a hardy gal who takes the place of her twin brother to bring in her man, and is blinded and lost in a dense forest during a snowstorm. Texas was "looking forward" to working in Canada. She was appalled when she learned that several cedar trees planted on the Triangle lot overlooking Santa Monica Bay were to represent the great Northwest! "When I inquired what they intended to do about the snowstorm, I was informed that the studio had a few hundred barrels of salt left over from a previous production."

She flew into a rage. "When I asked if they thought I could act with a few scattered cedar trees and a hundred barrels of salt, the director expressed himself as being in doubt as to my ability to act with a whole forest of cedars . . . Somehow my hand found an ink well, and I let fly one of those twirlers which have made so many baseball pitchers famous."

The ink well allegedly found its mark, and a different director completed *The Hellcat*. It was also the last western that Texas made for Triangle.

For more than a year, trouble had been hounding the corporation. Exhibitor rental fees were nearly exorbitant, from which Triangle skimmed off thirty-five percent of the gross and permitted no theater not under a Triangle contract to play its products. The New York Motion Picture Company (which now included Domino, Broncho, Keystone, and Kay-Bee) sold its interests and the negatives of many releases to Aitken. Shortly afterward, Griffith quit Triangle.

Aitken soon discovered that he had purchased a lot of contracts with overpaid Broadway performers who could only bleed him dry. He declined to come to terms with William S. Hart, and Hart unhappily left Triangle. So did Douglas Fairbanks. Allan Dawn was moved to the East Coast studio at Yonkers to complete the remaining productions of the firm with less impressive casts of players. In 1919 Aitken closed down Triangle's operations, sold most of its remaining assets to Adolph Zukor, and retired.

Texas Guinan went on to appear in *The Love Defender* (with Madge Evans and child character Dolly Meredith), directed by Tefft Johnson and released in March 1918 by World Films. Two months later, the *Moving Picture World* ran a double-page announcement that she had signed with the Frohman Amusement Corporation of Flushing, New York, for "twenty-six two-reel dramatic features typifying the glories and hazards of the women of the Great West . . . to be released one every two weeks commencing May 10, on the State Right basis . . . each story written by a separate author of prominence especially for Miss Guinan and directed by Cliff Smith," who had "achieved an excellent record" in western pictures.

This was only the beginning of the Guinan publicity.

The 1919 announcement by Frohman Amusement Corporation that Texas Guinan would appear in 26 two-reel feature productions "typifying the rights, glories and hazards of the women of the Great West."

Desirous of improving her own performances, Texas Guinan studied vaudeville's leading single women stars like Eva Tanguay, shown here in "Salome."

Another single woman star to catch Texas Guinan's attention was Mae West. As a Paramount star, she had already laid her curves on the couch and purred in her tantalizing drawl: "Come up and see me sometime."

Franchise advertisement on first five of the eight Guinan films produced by Victor Kremer Film Features, Inc., in 1921.

Two-gun Texas Guinan is shown here having the best of a nasty argument with a pair of culprits in Get-Away Kate (Triangle, 1917).

Francis Ford and Texas Guinan in scene from The Gun Woman *(Triangle, 1918).*

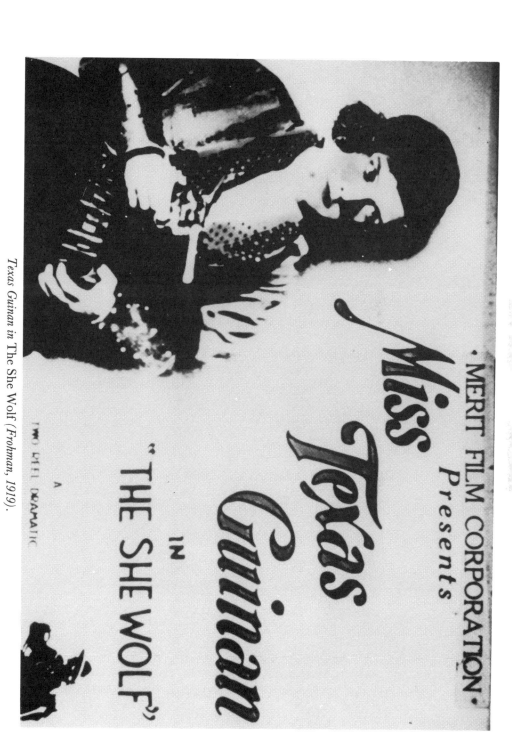

Texas Guinan in The She Wolf *(Frohman, 1919).*

Texas Guinan in "The She Wolf," a Frohman Amusement Two-Reeler, Looks Like an Honest-to-Goodness Gun Lady. "The She Wolf" is one of a series of Western two-reel features being made under the direction of William L. Sherrill, seen on the right with his company on location.

Scenes from The She Wolf *and production company on location (Frohman, 1919).*

Texas Guinan as Little Miss Deputy *(Frohman, 1919)*.

In one of her lighter moments during the filming of Little Miss Deputy.

Texas Guinan as Malamute Meg *(Frohman, 1919)*.

Texas Guinan in a scene from The Girl from Hell's Agony *(Frohman, 1919)*.

Victor Kremer Takes Out $500,000 Insurance on Texas Guinan Series

Due to an accident that came near causing the death of his star, Texas Guinan, Victor Kremer, president of the Victor Kremer Film Features, Inc., has taken out an unusually large insurance policy.

The accident in question happened last week when Miss Guinan, in making a leap over a cliff in her first picture, "I Am the Woman," was unseated by her horse and thrown headlong down the side of a hill.

The scene was being "shot'" under the direction of Francis Ford on a location near Los Angeles, the horse loosened a shoe, with the result that when Miss Guinan went over the cliff her charge fouled some obstacle and brought her "a cropper," nearly causing her serious injuries.

As a consequence Kremer decided that a repetition of such an accident might mean the interruption of the series of eight pictures which Miss Guinan is contracted for, and accordingly arranged to protect the same by a policy that would preclude the possibility of any loss by insurance.

The series which is to be released at the rate of two a month, commencing about March first, involved a large amount.

It is said no one company would assume the entire burden, so it was found necessary to divide the amount among several concerns. It was decided after several conferences to have issued separate policies on each of the eight pictures, each policy calling for a payment of $50,000 in case of an accident. This resolved itself into there being written eight policies, each in the amount of $50,000, or $400,000 for the whole.

Inasmuch as there were others who might be injured in the making of the pictures an additional policy of $100,000 was written to protect such members of the company who might meet with some accident that would call for the delay of the delivery, or release of any one of the series.

Totaled the amount of insurance called for to protect the release of the series on time is said to be one of the largest on record.

Kremer Film Features, Inc. takes out $500,000 insurance against accidental injury of Texas Guinan and other members of company in production of Guinan series (February 1921).

Texas Guinan in a scene from The Girl of the Rancho (*Bulls Eye-Reelcraft picture, 1920*).

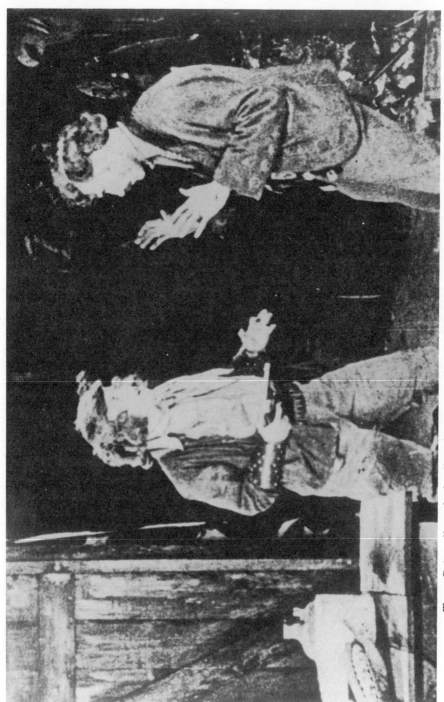

Texas Guinan "gets the drop" on the vicious outlaw El Tigre prior to "branding" him, in Letters of Fire (Bulls Eye-Reelcraft picture, 1920).

Texas Guinan to the rescue (with a club) in scene from The Boss of the Rancho *(Kremer, 1921).*

Texas Guinan and Francis Ford in scene from The Stampede *(Kremer, 1921)*.

The Stampede.

Autographed photo of Texas Guinan used on gummed, perforated publicity "stamps" (1921–1922).

CHAPTER 4

Texas Guinan Productions

The Frohman Corporation allowed that Guinan was the "most compelling, original and captivating character of the screen"; that "she came out of the vast unknown regions of the west with the spirit of the desert and the plains, the power and the brawn of those compelled to defend their own by force of might and will — and yet possessed all the graces and charms of a woman." The productions, being filmed at the Frohman West Coast studio, were to be "exploited as entertainments unto themselves and establish a new high water mark in Photo-Dramatic Creation."

Jesse J. Goldburg, general manager of the company, said: "Anyone who imagines the art of photoplay has reached its zenith will awaken to the fact that there are things yet to be done that will lift the motion picture beyond what it now stands for. The ingenue, sweet and bewitching always will be with us, but the day of the woman of brawn and brains is about to break upon the horizon."

President William L. Sherrill was so pleased with "the work already accomplished" that he was "determined to go further than originally contemplated" and believed "the showing of the first few releases will establish Miss Guinan as one of the most popular characters in filmdom . . . If any five- or six-reel Western productions can show more punch, greater detail, more extravagant sets or more beauty than the Texas Guinan Westerns, we have failed in our mission."

Buyers and exhibitors were no less enthusiastic. Before the first cameras ceased cranking, "many territories had been contracted" and others were being awarded contracts "in the order of receipt of acceptance."

Guinan's first Frohman offering was based on a story by John F. Colton entitled *The She Wolf*. Her supporting players were Josie Sedgwick, later the heroine of several Blue Streak Westerns for Universal, and Jack Richardson, hero of many 1915–16 Mustang two-reelers such as *Breezy Bill-Outcast, El Diablo, Man to Man,* and *Broadcloth and Buckskin*. George Chesebro was the bad guy, and Ah Wing, the great Chinese dramatic actor, was cast as the owner of a dancehall.

Director Cliff Smith was instructed to "proceed without regard to length." The 6,700 feet of film shot formed such a "powerful production" that it seemed impracticable to cut it to two reels. It cost nearly twice what the company was receiving for the rights of each two-reel production, and President Sherrill tentatively considered releasing it as a Texas Guinan Special.

The She Wolf was finally cut to five reels and released to exchanges under the financial terms of the regular two-reel Guinan contract. Letters poured in commending the company's policy.

The *Moving Picture World* of August 16, 1919, announced completion of three more Guinan westerns: *Some Gal, The Dangerous Little Devil,* and *Little Miss Deputy*. "These two-reelers present Texas Guinan as the straight shooting heroine with a punch in her gauntlet and a snap in her rawhide whip . . . possess all the popular Western features, cattle ranches, hard riding casts and heavy villains . . . A house strong for Western stories would do well to play these productions."

In *Some Gal,* Texas battles a sinister Mexican cattle thief named Juan Lopez, portrayed by Jack Richardson. The heroine's father, at the Mexican's mercy, tries to force his daughter to marry the thief, but Texas frustrates the plot.

She later remembered the stunt of the picture: "We loosed one hundred wild west ponies from a corral . . . A three year old boy was playing in the middle of the road. I saw this from a hill and my part was to cut in and pick up the child. When I saw those horses bearing down on that child and I knew I *had* to get him — we couldn't fake it — my whole body felt numb and my blood seemed frozen . . . I was so frightened I nearly missed."

Texas as *The Dangerous Little Devil* (so-called because of the fighting qualities she displays without invitation) saves, by hard riding, a dam controlling the water supply of the valley and owned by the hero. It was the second time that she had a scare: "I was tearing down a hill and the boys had ridden me off to the side. Suddenly I saw a tree with a very low limb. I couldn't miss it by lying low on the horse's back, so I swung under the horse and hung to the belly strap of the saddle. My cameraman, Elmer Dan, who up to that time had never failed, was so frightened he stopped shooting."

Little Miss Deputy was one of Guinan's best pictures. Playing the part of a deputy sheriff, she is placed in a situation where she must either renounce her womanhood and hang the man she loves or take off her badge. She proves that the hero has been wrongly accused and saves him at the critical moment.

Guinan made four other pictures for Frohman in 1919: *South of Santa Fe, Malamute Meg, The Girl of Hell's Agony* (a five-reeler), and *The Dead Man's Hand,* with Richardson, Sedgwick, Chesebro, Leo Willis, Billie Bennett, H. M. Dudgeon, and Cliff Smith himself in various casts. *Dead Man's Hand,* which promoted Texas as "The Female Bill Hart of the Screen," was written by husband Julian Johnson and directed by Francis J. Grandon.

Cliff Smith had organized his own production company, and the existence of the Frohman Amusement Corporation (which survived longer than most independents) came rapidly to a close. Guinan's other projected films were not completed.

Texas and Julian Johnson also dissolved their partnership. She gave no reason for their divorce in 1920, only saying: "He was my idea of a good scout, a regular guy. As husbands went he was all right — and he went!" Shortly afterwards, she married a George E. Townley, whom she had known only briefly. They soon separated.

The same year, Texas signed for another twenty-six two-reel westerns with Bull's Eye Film Corporation, distributing through Reelcraft Pictures Corporation of Los Angeles.

In June, Reelcraft announced a state right sale for *The White Squaw, The Night Rider,* and a remake of her earlier production, *The Wildcat. Moving Picture World* of October 2, 1920, noted the release of *The Desert Vulture* and *The Girl of the Rancho.* Soon added to her Bull's Eye output were *Call of Bob White, My Lady Robin Hood,* and a feature, *Letters of Fire*. Imaginatively titled, with plots that moved swiftly and violently with no gray between good and evil, the series brought Texas the attention she desired.

Letters of Fire was the best publicized and a favorite of exhibitors. Texas, the sheriff, is framed by a vicious outlaw, El Tigre, to cover up his cattle rustling activity. Placed in a bad light with her once staunch constituents, Texas takes the outlaw's trail and catches his henchmen red-handed. She is surprised and captured in turn by El Tigre, who for her audacity brands his initials on her bosom before turning her loose. Making her way to the home of a friendly Mexican woman, Texas recuperates from her pain and humiliation and again sets out to bring El Tigre to justice. She does so in a slam-bang climax, repaying him in kind by branding his chest with *her* initials before being pulled off by the posse which arrives to help round up the rustlers.

Texas remembered one hair-raising stunt at the finish: "The boys [in the posse] were sure shots and I could depend on them . . . As I jumped from the limb of a tree, the villain roped me around the neck, to hang me. There was no faking this scene . . . my life actually depended on one of the boys, Dutch McCraken, shooting the rope in two, thus allowing me to land on the back of my horse and make a get-away."

Texas enjoyed more than modest success at Bull's Eye, but her experience was hardly satisfying. Directors complained about her exaggerated gestures and Bill Hart grimaces — screen acting techniques that had been obsolete for years. Her tough, hard-bitten appearance on-screen and painfully revealing close-ups (she was now thirty-six and quite stocky) rendered her far from being the attractive heroine a new generation of fans desired. Texas charged she had not been paid the full percentage due her from her films. Reelcraft maintained that her pictures were playing the cheaper houses, and revenues were far short of the amounts anticipated.

Bull's Eye suspended work on her remaining eighteen films. "Reneged on their contract," Texas put it. She left Bull's Eye, but was undeterred.

In January 1921, she appeared in *Not Guilty* for First National, then signed with Victor Kremer Film Features, Inc., of New York for a series of eight five-reel western dramas to be directed by her former co-star at Triangle, Francis Ford. Her first Kremer production, *I Am the Woman,* was shot in early February, near Los Angeles.

In one scene Texas was about to leap from a cliff when her horse loosened a shoe. "In making the leap, Miss Guinan was unseated and thrown headlong down the side of the hill, nearly causing her serious injuries."

Moving Picture World of February 12 noted the incident and reported:

> The eight pictures which Miss Guinan is contracted for ... involves a large amount. As a consequence Victor Kremer, president of Victor Kremer Film Features, Inc., decided that a repetition of such an accident might mean interruption of the series ... and accordingly arranged to protect the members by insurance ...
>
> No company would assume the entire burden so it became necessary to divide the amount among several concerns ... a policy of $50,000 on each of the eight pictures, or $400,000 for the whole. An additional policy of $100,000 was written to protect the company from accident that might delay the delivery or release of any one of the series ... The $500,000 amount called for is said to be one of the largest on record.

This was great publicity for the series. By mid-April, *I Am the Woman* had been franchised in New York, Philadelphia, Atlanta, New Orleans, and Dallas, with requests from other territories arriving daily. Six more Guinan features were completed by July: *The Girl Sheriff, The School M'arm, Redhead, The Wild Flower of the Mountain Range, The Boss of the Rancho,* and *The Stampede.*

The Stampede was adapted by Kingsley Benedict from a story by Eugenie Kremer. Its cast was: Guinan (Tex Henderson), Francis Ford (Robert Wagner), Frederick Moore (Jim Henderson, Tex's father), Jean Carpenter (Mary, Wagner's motherless daughter), Fred Kohler (Steve Norton), Cecil McLean (Sylvia Dean, Tex's cousin), Kingsley Benedict (Beauty Anders), Snowflake (Tex's horse), and Vale Rio (Snowflake's trainer).

No information about the precise nature of these films is available. If an eighth feature was made, its title is unknown.

Meanwhile, Texas instituted a suit against Reelcraft Pictures Corporation for $200,000 which she claimed was still owed her. The settlement was not disclosed. It appears to have been an effort to raise production capital. In August 1921, she organized Texas Guinan Productions to try her own hand at making and starring in a series of two-reel western and northwestern pictures. She was supported in this venture by Frohman's former manager, Jesse Goldburg.

Guinan summarized it as follows: "I got twelve real cowboys, a scenario writer [Mildred Sledge], a cameraman, a carload of cartridges, my horse 'Waco' from Texas [which she had trained personally and boasted could do *anything* short of flying!], and went to work. We made a picture a week. Jay Hunt directed . . . only the dramatic scenes however, and left to me the riding and shooting. I certainly put over some hair raising stunts and I never had a double in one of my pictures, or even a dummy.

"I wanted lots of thrills . . . to please children . . . appeal to the small town people."

She allegedly produced more than 300 movies. Once asked how her scenarist managed to come up with so many different plots, she quipped: "We never changed plots — only the horses."

On the contrary, only a few of the Guinan titles are known: *The Spitfire, Across the Border, The Heart of Texas, Texas of the Mounted,* and *A Moonshine Feud.* Manager Goldburg arrived in Los Angeles on August 29 to commence production, with the first release scheduled for the state right market October 1. *Moving Picture World* of September 3 announced that a contract had been closed with I. E. Chadwick of the Merit Film Company of New York and Baltimore, "whereby the first twelve Texas Guinan two-reel productions were acquired for the territory of Greater New York and New York State, Northern New Jersey, Delaware, Maryland, District of Columbia and Virginia . . . From the large number of inquiries which continue to come in, officials of the company state that it will be only a brief time before the distribution of the series for the entire United States will be completed."

Texas recalled: "I sold and resold my pictures all over the world. They were tremendously popular in the Orient and South America. Marcus Loew bought them over five different times. I went all over the country with Loew when he opened his string of movie theaters and appeared in person with my cowboys and horse 'Waco.' "

She also did well with vending machine cards and perforated gummed stamps which featured reductions of her various photos and were used like Easter seals on advertisements and correspondence sent to exchanges and exhibitors through the U.S. mail.

But the day of "quickie" westerns was waning. America had entered a decade of happy escape from the postwar rigors of reform and problem solving. The Eighteenth Amendment to the Constitution, designed to eradicate the evils of the saloon and intemperance, and the Prohibition Enforcement Act (the enforcement apparatus for the amendment) which went into effect in January 1920, had ushered in a new era of vicious institutions. Road houses, speakeasies, beer flats, and blind pigs flourished because of an open contempt for the law by their proprietors and patrons. Their existence encouraged illicit liquor traffic, hijacking, gang wars, and official corruption. The automobile was more readily available. The national craze was night club partying and highball sipping, daring clothes, sensual jazz and new dance steps which preachers denounced to their flocks as lascivious. Texas Guinan, a ripe thirty-eight but with plenty of gusto and lung power, wanted a piece of the action.

New York called. In 1922, Texas folded her Hollywood company and answered.

CHAPTER 5

Prohibition and Broadway

In 1923, Texas was back on Broadway. Much publicized as a vaudeville trouper and gun heroine of the western screen, she played in a musical production at the Winter Garden.

Following one evening performance, she attended a social gathering of showfolk in the lounge of the Beaux Arts Hotel. She recalled: "It was a dull affair. Someone suggested that I sing. I didn't need much coaxing, so I sang all I knew — my entire repertoire. First thing you know we were all doing things. Everybody had a great time."

The hotel manager was so pleased that he insisted she accept a post as mistress of ceremonies. In this role, Texas delighted customers with her ebullience and salty repartee. She also caught the attention of a horse-faced dandy, Larry Fay, sometime entrepreneur, sometime racketeer.

Fay's career spanned some forty arrests — for nothing more serious than offending the peace and dignity of the city — and interests ranging from a legitimate taxicab fleet to clip joint bootlegging to a muscle-man setup that preyed on wholesale dairymen and rigged milk prices. He also operated an emporium, the El Fey Club, with a swastika on the entrance wall for a good luck emblem.

45

He had copied the symbol from a horse blanket long before Adolph Hitler made it a hated one.

Fay recognized the commercial possibilities of a performer-hostess who would trade insults with patrons, maintain an atmosphere of camaraderie, and spur thrill-seeking, out-of-town buyers to the heights of expenditure. He talked it over with Texas Guinan. Texas suggested a partnership. Fay agreed and set her up at the El Fey Club. Thus began a profitable relationship that established Guinan as one of the brightest lights on the Great White Way.

By 1924 the great bulk of New York's cabaret customers had been lost to the new and highly informal competitor, the night club, where "members" paid a stiff cover charge plus charges for every accessory item. These customers thumbed their noses at prohibition, dined, danced, viewed the Shimmy (cooch) or jazz (jazzing) performers, and stayed as long as they cared to throw around their folding money.

More astounding was the growth of the openly illicit, much raided, padlocked in vain speakeasy. Thousands of speakeasies had replaced the old Raines-law hotel and corner saloon, and all you had to do for admittance was to knock twice on a sliding panel behind an iron grill or ring a bell in a special way and tell the cautious face which appeared in the open portal that "Joe sent me."

New York, in fact, was an oasis of speaks in basements of fashionable mansions, in penthouses, brownstone rooming houses, tenements, office buildings, stores, restaurants, and tea rooms. It was said that one could get a drink in any building on Fifty-second Street between Fifth and Sixth avenues; that Forty-fifth Street (in the so-called "Broadway Forties") was the wettest street in America.

Speakeasies also provided the fundamental of New York nightlife — sex. For the lonelier clients, there was anything from "hostesses," cigarette and checkroom girls, to hideaway mistresses, to simple hustlers.

New York police viewed the speaks as primarily a federal responsibility, but the Prohibition Bureau assigned only 200 dry agents (for the most part inefficient and underpaid political employees) to ferret out the thousands of "traps" in the sprawling metropolis of six million people.

In the fierce competition for business, entertainment and personalities were economic necessities. Into her venture, said the *New York Times*, Texas Guinan "introduced the technique of familiarity and bonhomie that remained her stock-in-trade until her death. The loud, cheerful, full-throated 'Hello, sucker!' that greeted her patrons, a mixed consistory of out-of-town buyers, theatrical celebrities and a sprinkling of the social and underworld elite, became a national vogue." Seated on a tall stool in the center of the main room, dominating the nightly bedlam and armed with a clapper-type noisemaker or a police whistle, or both, she "wisecracked and quipped" and made her customers willing to be overcharged and happy. "Never at a loss for a retort discourteous, it was her custom to encourage heckling rather than frown upon it."

Nitery singers enjoyed their "biggest vogue." Texas Guinan's singing voice was "no great shakes," but her personality made her the best-known name of all the fabulous Broadway hostesses. As *Variety* commented, "Galli-Curci would flop in a nite club . . . yet Tex knocks out three grand [monthly] for her bit, all through the knack of hammering a socially prominent patron on the cranium with a kleeter-klapper clapper. The others flock to her museum of unnatural hysterics to see 'em take that treatment on the 'nut' religiously, and apparently relish it."

Writer Edmund Wilson, who knew the Jazz Age well, referred to Guinan as "this prodigious woman, with her pearls, her glittering bosom, her abundant beautifully bleached coiffure, her formidable trap of shining white teeth, her broad bare back behind its grating of green velvet, the full-blown peony as big as a cabbage exploding on her broad green thigh."

Texas denied that she sold liquor, only set-ups for customers who brought their own. Yet she did a brisk business in Scotch and champagne at $25 a bottle when reasonably certain that the feds were not around. She featured pretty girls — lots of them. Their high kicks, wiggles, and other charms helped distract customers from the price of booze. Though a singer or dancer in one of her shows might have only a modicum of talent, when Texas commanded, "Give the little girl a great big hand!" the little girl got just that. It was also her closing line for the chorus, "Give the little girls a great big hand!"

She was topped only once. A dry agent arose from the audience, placed his hand on her shoulder, and called to a fellow agent: "Give this little girl a great big handcuff." It was her first pinch.

Texas took it in good grace. She laughed with the crowd while the El Fey Club was raided by the feds and a police prohibition squad. She appeared briefly in court, the premises were padlocked, and a few days later she was again "packing them in like sardines" at a new establishment, the Del Fay Club, just two blocks from the old.

The Del Fay, too, was soon forced to close. Said the *Times:* "After federal agents, fortified with writs and warrants, haled her into court . . . the indefatigable hostess moved into the Texas Guinan Club at 117 West Forty-eighth Street . . . and her coterie willingly followed . . .

"It was there that a 'live one' appeared one night, paid the couvert [cover] charge, distributed $50 bills among the entertainers, and for his bounty received as a title the most famous phrase in the Guinan nomenclature. He refused to reveal his name but remarked that he was in 'the dairy produce business,' so the stranger was introduced from the floor as 'A Big Butter-and-Egg Man.' "

Thereafter, the phrase was used to refer to a big spender.

Many stories emanated from the Texas Guinan Club:

One typical butter-and-egg man claimed that it cost him $1,000 to fix a cigarette lighter in the club. His girlfriend's lighter wouldn't work; he took it apart and accidentally spilled some of the fluid on her expensive fur coat. A lighted cigarette set the coat on fire, and waiters finished ruining it with a fire extinguisher. The $1,000 the jolly spender complained about was the price of a new coat.

When a man at a ringside table moaned to the doll sitting with him, "I feel terrible — I lost $337,000 in the market today," a waiter serving an adjoining table said, contemptuously: "These drunks will cry over any little thing."

Another illegally stimulated patron still in the club at 3:00 A.M. swore that he had watched a nude dancer do an exotic version of Leda and the Swan with a sleepy, eight-foot boa constrictor.

Such stories and Guinan's antics caught the attention of B. P. Schulberg, former Connecticut journalist and scenario editor who had become head of production at Paramount Pictures. By request, Texas reported to Paramount studios to appear as herself in Allan Dawn's presentation of *Night Life in New York*, casting Rod La-Rocque, Ernest Torrence, Dorothy Gish, Helen Lee Worthing, and George Hackethorne. Incidentally, the title editor was Texas's ex-husband, Julian Johnson.

"A light, bright, 'bright-light' picture, *Night Life* is enough 'hokey' to make it appealing, possibly more so for the hinterland which will . . . wonder at the erotic and exotic aura of the supper clubs and secretly envy but hypocritically voice their conclusions," said *Variety*.

Night Life played the Rivoli Theater in New York the week of July 12, 1924. Meanwhile, the feds and police squads swept down on no less than thirty Broadway night spots. The Texas Guinan Club was among those forced to turn out the lights.

Texas didn't feel too badly. She saw it only as a temporary inconvenience. "Where in hell would I be without prohibition?" she asked when the agents flashed their badges. As they carried her away, she had the band strike up "The Prisoner's Song."

Seventeen night spot owners were indicted for alleged conspiracy to violate the prohibition laws and ordered held for trial in federal court by Judge Augustus N. Hand. A few pleaded guilty to transporting distilled, denatured alcohol and were fined $500 each. One club was ordered closed for three months.

On August 4, Texas and her attorney, Harold Content, called on Assistant United States Attorney Frederic C. Bellinger. Texas vehemently denied any knowledge that liquor was being sold in the Guinan establishment, and her claim that she was only an employee in the place was never successfully disproved. Later, Larry Fay appeared with Herman Wise, counsel for the club, and admitted he owned stock in it. Texas asked that no permanent injunction be issued against herself. The club was closed for six months. Texas capitalized on the publicity value of the raid by wearing a necklace of little gold padlocks and a diamond bracelet from which dangled a small gold police whistle.

She also took time out, because of the lengthy separation, to divorce George Townley, her last husband. In late August, she went to Florida, still in partnership with Larry Fay, and set up the Miami Del Fey Club.

The *New York Times* noted: "Striking the high mark of the Florida real estate boom, the venture was a bonanza. The profits were enormous.

"So conspicuous was the Guinan-Fay success that both were hounded by real estate brokers, hoping for a quick turnover. Miss Guinan had an answer that repulsed all advances:

" 'Listen, suckers. You take them by the sun. I take them by the moon. Now, let's don't interfere with each other's business.' "

Fay disagreed. Their relationship deteriorated, and in December 1925, Texas returned to New York. In January 1926 she opened the 300 Club at 151 West Fifty-fourth Street, and with her "old gang of seventy-eight," the same general prices and imposing cover charges, soon put the new establishment well in the black.

CHAPTER 6

A Brush With Mrs. Willebrandt

Despite her apparent irreverence — and casual attitude toward husbands — Texas was devoted to family and friends. She watched over her girls like a mother lion protecting her cubs, and brought her aging father and mother and younger brother Tommy to New York to live with her in a lavish thirty-two-room flat she occupied on West Eighth Street. The place was also populated with an assortment of parrots, dogs, and cats. She provided her father employment at the 300 Club.

Texas showed as much charity toward her business competitors. One of these was Belle Livingston. In her showgirl days before the turn of the century, Belle was billed as the Kansas Sunshine Baby with "the poetic legs." Six feet tall, weighing nearly 175 pounds, she served as her own bouncer and once tried to throw out a squad of dry agents who were raiding her place. Unlike Guinan's intimate, crowded, noisy 300 Club, Belle's fashionable Country Palace on Fifty-eighth Street offered everything from bars, grill-rooms, and private rooms to ping-pong and a miniature golf course. One floor was decorated in a Japanese motif, where customers sat Oriental-style on expensive cushions and quenched their thirst. Belle's reason? "A man could get hurt falling off a bar stool," she said.

While Texas tried to get along with the feds, Belle fought them and got into trouble. Belle often discussed her plight with Texas over a cup of coffee, and after she served time in jail for purveying bootleg whiskey, Texas sent an armored car to escort her back to the Great White Way.

Guinan's one rival, both in business and personality, was Helen Morgan. The husky-voiced torch singer with sad eyes and a ragged mop of hair had starred in movies and musical comedies. But she is best remembered perched on a piano in her Summer Home at 134 West Fifty-second Street, wringing her handkerchief and wailing "Bill," "Why Was I Born," and "Can't Help Lovin' Dat Man." Customers went to Guinan's club for laughs and horse-play; they went to Helen Morgan's Summer Home to sip liquor in the foul air and clouds of tobacco smoke and let the tears roll down their cheeks.

In February 1926 the police department initiated another tactic in its war on night clubs. Police Commissioner George V. Mc-Laughlin, in cooperation with the Bureau of Buildings, launched a campaign to "effectually end the illegal activities of establishments conspicuous in the night life of the city where building ordinances were being violated." On February 8 representatives of Texas Guinan's club and the Melody Club at 114 West Fifty-fourth Street were haled into Magistrate Harry A. Gordon's West Side Court charged with "violating the building ordinances in the operation of dancing."

Capt. Charles B. Burns and Patrolman Maurice Coffey of the West Forty-seventh Street Station, and John O. Lewis, an inspector from the building bureau, testified that Guinan's club contained 200 persons at 2:00 A.M. on Sunday, February 7, when the summons was served; that her certificate of occupancy "permitted but 75 to be there at one time, and in case of fire, not more than that number could leave safely with the existing facilities for exit."

Louis Stillman, counsel for the club, pointed out that it was on the ground floor, which was of concrete, and promised to see that another exit was provided immediately.

"If your certificate calls for but 75 persons, that is all I will tolerate," Magistrate Gordon said.

The *Times* of February 9 noted: "Guinan's club was running last night, but the police reported that it was being conducted in compliance with the law."

The Melody Club, operating over a garage, without a certificate of occupancy, did not fare so well. Inspector Lewis told the court a certificate would never be granted because the location made it too dangerous for dancers. "The Melody was dark last night," the *Times* continued. "A sign on the door said: 'Closed during alterations.' "

Moving against the speakeasies, Commissioner McLaughlin enlisted the aid of the fire department. Many speaks were equipped with steel doors and barred windows, contrary to fire regulations. McLaughlin vowed to obtain proof of every violation and, if necessary, station patrolmen on the premises "to guard against further infringements."

The campaign took a bite out of the 300 Club's business. To compensate for the loss, Texas set up her brother in Texas Tommy Guinan's Playground (second and third floors) at 201 West Fifty-second Street. Other clubs solved their problem by relocating; many speakeasies moved to new locations and had to be "ferreted out" again. Their numbers even increased. For the most part, Commissioner McLaughlin's campaign was in vain.

At 3:00 A.M. on Sunday, July 4, the police and prohibition agents swept down on the 300 Club in the most spectacular and well-publicized raid ever conducted against a Guinan establishment. Among the guests present were two dozen members of the Georgia delegation to welcome Bobby Jones, who had returned to the United States on Friday after winning the British golf championship, several of the golfing party, and two United States senators. Jones himself was not present.

The agents and detectives entered the club quietly, presented a search warrant, and announced their identity from the center of the dance floor. The 400 patrons, upon realizing the nature of the visit, were "thrown into confusion." Some became "very boisterous . . . offered to fight it out man to man," and about twenty were "forcibly ejected." According to employee Michael Guinan, the police went "roughly" among the guests, many of whom "expressed indignation at what they termed an unwarranted intrusion."

Several asked to be arrested. Only two were taken into custody: Julia Dunn, a seventeen-year-old entertainer, for having taken part in an objectionable dance, and Hyman Edson, the club manager, for having permitted the dance. Spirits seized were minimal: two bottles of gin, one of rye, and one of Scotch whiskey. Representatives of the club who followed the police and their prisoners to the West Forty-seventh Street Station denied that liquor had been found there. It had been found, the police said, in a room built out from the kitchen.

Michael Guinan testified: "We do not have to sell liquor. We get $6 from every person who sits down at one of our tables. This is for cover charges, and ginger ale at $1.50 a glass."

Magistrate Albert Vitale dismissed the liquor charges for lack of evidence.

Policewomen Margaret Solan and Margaret Leonard, dressed as flappers seeking a thrill, and Detectives Charles Wand and George Creed, in evening clothes posing as big spenders, had visited the club for several nights to obtain the information upon which the raid warrant was issued. Policewoman Solan testified she had entered the club after midnight; that shortly Miss Dunn appeared in flesh-colored tights trimmed with imitation pearl beads and moved among the tables dancing. Solan exhibited an item "not more than six inches in length and three in width," which she said constituted "the whole of the dancer's costume." Miss Dunn explained that because of the position of the tables in the 300 Club she had been forced to dance very close to the patrons.

Magistrate Vitale dismissed the complaints against Dunn and Edson upon motion of their attorney.

Club patrons were critical of the police for what they termed a "grand stand play" and insisted that the police had been "tipped off that the prominent out-of-town persons were to be present." The police declared they knew nothing of the so-called "Bobby Jones night."

The *Times* concluded its July 4 report: "This is the first case in which members of the New York Police Department have been sent out to obtain evidence of prohibition law violation with the privilege of spending as much money as is required to become known as a 'good spender' at places as high priced as the 300 Club."

Texas Guinan declined public comment, but continued to spoof the feds. Later that year, she had an opportunity to barb the work of the assistant attorney general in the United States Department of Justice. Mrs. Mabel Walker Willebrandt.

Mrs. Willebrandt, a native Kansan and a lawyer, in charge of cases under federal tax and prohibition laws, had not taken her duties lightly. She inquired into liquor conditions in many sections of the country and the part played by the American judiciary in creating them as described by those who registered their reactions to the government. She personally led speakeasy raids, brought a boom to the padlock industry, and seemed to take special delight in putting the squeeze on operators like Texas Guinan.

In 1926, Baylor University in Waco decided to confer upon Mrs. Willebrandt an honorary degree.

Veteran New York newsman Emery Winn, then a cub reporter on the Waco *Times-Herald,* recalled: "The managing editor of the Waco papers was a person of great imagination who had an uncanny ability to pick out ideas that would stir up some talk. Why not wire Miss Guinan in New York and have her send a greeting to Mrs. Willebrandt to be published upon her arrival? Wasn't Miss Guinan a native of Waco? And who knew Mrs. Willebrandt better than Texas Guinan? So the managing editor sent the wire. Then he assigned me to interview Mrs. Willebrandt when she pulled in . . ."

Texas Guinan's reply was a "humdinger." In general, she was "so happy that Mrs. Willebrandt was visiting Waco where she would meet some of the finest people in the world . . . people who minded their own business and didn't go around poking their noses into other folks' affairs."

Reporter Winn turned in his interview, and the managing editor ran it and the Guinan article "side by side . . . in a big page one display." Hundreds of Waco citizens were outraged. Since the interview carried Winn's byline, he bore the brunt of the criticism. In time, of course, it was generally forgotten. And Mrs. Willebrandt got her revenge of sorts.

At 10:00 the night of December 21, from his office in the Federal Building in New York, United States District Attorney Emory R. Buckner launched the most sweeping drive yet undertaken to stem the high tide of liquor, with its promise of a wet Christmas and a wetter New Year. Seven raiding parties, each made up of policemen, prohibition agents, assistant United States attorneys and deputy United States marshals, served padlock complaint bills and temporary personal injunctions upon the proprietors of fifty-eight night clubs, cabarets, and other resorts in Manhattan.

The *Times* of December 22 provided this summary:

"Among the places visited were some of the city's most glittering centers of night life, where the cost of an evening or an early morning conviviality is as heavy as the depression of the morning after . . . To gain evidence against the most 'exclusive' of such places investigators posed as wealthy Englishmen and, in at least one instance, as a Russian nobleman, and were introduced by prominent persons, among whom were well-known Broadwayites and a leading woman in a successful theatrical production."

U.S. Attorney Buckner added: "So thoroughly did these polished prohibition agents worm their way into the good graces of Broadwayites that Texas Guinan, on their second visit to her 300 Club, threw them a kiss and asked why they were leaving so early."

Among the other fifty-seven establishments falling to the injunction drive were Texas Tommy Guinan's Playground and the Del Fay Club reactivated by Larry Fay.

Texas insisted (as always) that she didn't have to sell hard liquor because she got as much for a pitcher of ice or sparkling water as people paid for Scotch before Prohibition. "Customers bring their own whiskey — on their hips. So what can I do except provide set-ups?" The evidence was sufficient, however. On December 22, Capt. John W. Inglesby, head of the prohibition service padlock division, posted a preliminary injunction on the door of the 300 Club "restraining the corporation and all its officers" from further violations of the Volstead Act.

The club remained open, and to keep her customers in high spirits, Texas sang this ditty:

> *The Judge said, "Tex, do you sell booze?"*
> *I said, "Please, don't be silly.*
> *I swear to you my cellar's filled*
> *With chocolate and vanilly."*

On January 14, Texas entertained at "one of the most sumptuous and elaborate parties in recent New York life." The Lyres Club, comprising leaders in industry, held its twentieth annual revel at the Hotel Ambassador. Among the guests were officers of several large railroads, including the Southern Pacific, New York Central, Long Island, and the Nickel Plate. Others present were the vice-president of American Telephone and Telegraph, the vice-president of Consolidated Gas, and the presidents of Brooklyn Edison and the B.M.T.

The evening's celebration began with a private dinner in a main dining room on the Fifty-first Street side of the hotel, with short addresses by the president of the Interborough and others prominent in the city's business. Afterwards, the guests retired to the ballroom converted into a jungle of moss-hung palm trees, with doves flying among the branches and monkeys and parrots cavorting overhead. At one end was a sandy beach, bordered with palms.

The guests relaxed in swinging chairs hung from the lower branches of the trees and at tables shaded from the tropical sun and had their coffee and cigars. While they chatted, Texas Guinan, with a fifteen-girl chorus, her singers, comedians, and band, came tripping onto the beach. The girls wore beaded South Sea costumes and "danced about on the white sand . . . in a real Hawaiian scene."

The party broke up about midnight and Miss Guinan "led her corps of entertainers back to her club," the *Times* said. "With her she took an eighteen-inch silver loving cup engraved with an expression of the Lyres' gratitude."

CHAPTER 7

A Big Hand for
Aimee and the Feds

Despite the numerous raids and padlock decrees, Texas Guinan had never been long out of business nor personally suffered either fine or imprisonment. But her honeymoon with the feds was ending.

Dry agents Truman Fowler, J. Walter Longcope, and Palmer Tubbs spent several hours in the 300 Club the evening of February 17, 1927, posing as big spenders and merrymakers. They noted that a nod of Miss Guinan's head caused waiters promptly to eject any person who made himself objectionable. Also at a nod of her head, a patron who asked for liquor received it. Shortly before 3:00 A.M., the curfew hour, when the club was crowded with men and women, the orchestra was in full blast, and the entertainers were disporting on the dance floor, the agents were able to "establish a clear line of communication with the source of supply."

Fowler bought a pint of whiskey for $10, and sampled it. He left the table and slipped out the door. This was the cue for the raid. Capt. John Inglesby and half a dozen other agents waiting outside made a dash for the place.

Harry Litwin, the doorman, tried to prevent their entry, but one agent drew his pistol and ordered him to one side. Litwin obeyed and the agents made a quick search of the club. Captain Inglesby found the preliminary injunction he had posted on Decem-

58

ber 22 stuffed in a cuspidor. He stepped up to where Miss Guinan sat on her high stool with clapper in hand and informed her that she was under arrest.

Texas rose to the occasion. "What, again?" she asked. "I hope I can ride in a taxi." Captain Inglesby promised to oblige. Texas then called to Tommy Guinan, who was standing nearby: "Bring along $500. I might want to play poker at the station house." Throwing a rap over her evening gown, she walked outside with Inglesby.

Meanwhile, the other agents took into custody Manager Hyman Edson; John Golden, the waiter who had sold them the liquor; John Hagen, another waiter; and Litwin, the doorman. All were driven to the West Forty-seventh Street Station. A dozen of the entertainers, most of them scantily clad with fur coats thrown over their shoulders, and more than a hundred guests determined not to miss anything of the night's show piled into private cars or taxis and followed.

While those who could crowded into the narrow confines in front of Lt. Bernard McGowan's desk and the others milled on the sidewalk, Captain Inglesby charged Texas Guinan with possessing and selling liquor in violation of the prohibition act and Edson, Golden, Hagen, and Litwin with acting in concert. He then lodged against Miss Guinan an additional charge of contempt of court in disregarding the injunction issued against the club on December 22.

As to the question of bail, Inglesby told Lieutenant McGowan that none would be permitted unless ordered by a federal judge. McGowan asked Texas if there was anything she wanted before being taken to jail. "Yes," she replied, "give me a couple of Confessionals; they'll make good reading."

Edson, Golden, Hagen, and Litwin were arraigned before United States Commissioner Garrett W. Cotter in the Federal Building the morning of February 18 and released under $500 bail each. Attorney M. M. Edelstein appeared for the 300 Club and its hostess in the liquor violation and contempt proceedings before Federal District Judge William Bondy.

Assistant United States Attorney Lowell W. Wadmond explained that the contempt charge was a separate case against the club and those active in its management. Edelstein declared that Miss Guinan was not the owner of the club; that she had never been personally served with any injunction, and therefore could not

be held liable. Maj. Chester P. Mills, federal prohibition administrator in the New York district, maintained that Miss Guinan was
the known owner of the club, yet "always professes to be an inno-
cent, if not victimized employee." Edelstein submitted that she was
neither owner, part owner, nor manager, and the government had
not established that she derived income from that source apart
from her salary. The court sustained Mr. Edelstein.

Texas still faced the new charge of violating the prohibition
law. Shortly before noon, she was released on $1,000 bail to appear
with Hyman, Golden, Hagen, and Litwin for trial before U.S.
Commissioner Cotter on February 19.

Texas had returned to her club to prepare for the night's business when the California evangelist, Mrs. Aimee Semple Mc-
Pherson, arrived in New York on tour and addressed an overflow
afternoon crowd at the Glad Tidings Tabernacle on West Thirty-
third Street. Mrs. McPherson had attracted national attention and
a grand jury investigation by her recent disappearance from Los
Angeles, which she attributed to bandits who had kidnapped her.
She declared the stories that she had departed with a radio opera-
tor at the Angelus Temple, where she had conducted twenty services weekly, were created by political enemies.

Mrs. McPherson told her audience she had found a sentiment
throughout the country that "will culminate in a revival of the old
religion and a return to godliness." As the mother of a sixteen-year-
old girl, she "had confidence in youth" and thought the church was
"lagging badly" in its battle with the world. "The world is wearing
seven-league boots . . . the young folk are carried along by the
world's pace; the church trips along in slippers and must face the
problems."

She spoke on the evil of drinking, drunkards, the teaching of
evolution in schools as the substitution of prayer and God, while
her listeners responded in choruses of "yes, yes" and "praise the
Lord." She held aloft the Bible, "the book of chiming bells . . . of
tinkling streams," and told of the days when she thought it the dull-
est book she had ever read but now believed every word it held.
And she prayed that "this throbbing metropolis, home of the nation's greatest men, center of the greatest buildings and stores,
known for its great culture, will some day be blessed as the home of
the nation's greatest revival churches." In addition, she believed a
"clean up" of the theater in New York was "about due," and an-

nounced that, in the evening, she would tour its night clubs to study at close range "the lights that singe so many butterfly wings."

On her evening rounds, Mrs. McPherson stopped first at the Open Door on McDougal Street. She scanned the dancers crowded into a narrow, low-ceilinged room, writing her observations in a small notebook. Two men started a fight in front of her table but were quickly subdued by waiters.

By midnight she reached the 300 Club. Texas greeted her cordially. After considerable persuasion, Mrs. McPherson consented to being introduced from the center of the dance floor. She made a short talk on how she was "seeing a new side of New York," reminding those at the tables that "behind all these beautiful clothes, behind all these good times," there was "something else in life," and quoted: "What doth it profit a man if he gain the whole world and loses his soul."

She invited all present to attend her sermon at 2:30 P.M. on the morrow. Texas announced that she intended to hear Mrs. McPherson, and when she asked the guests how many of them would do likewise, there was "a shout of assent from all sides." As Mrs. McPherson turned to leave, Texas called out: "This is a woman I admire. She has the courage of her convictions. Give this little woman a great big hand!" And the guests did.

A snowstorm and sharp northeast winds the following day failed to keep the crowds away. Again the tabernacle auditorium was filled to capacity and hundreds braved the temperature outside and listened as amplifiers carried Mrs. McPherson's message. Prominent in the first crowd were Texas Guinan, her dancer Laura Wilkinson, and a dozen from her night show, who occupied seats in front and directly under the pulpit. Photographers crowded within the altar and exploded their flash bulbs, until the evangelist asked them to desist.

Mrs. McPherson referred to night clubs and theaters as "among the things that fail to satisfy." Her text was from the Songs of Solomon, Chapter 2, "I Am the Rose of Sharon." Her evangelical appeals were impromptu. "Prayer and the Bible give them to me," she said. "I read the Bible and the word of God flows back into me . . . I wind up like a phonograph record, then I go to a meeting and preach and it goes the other way. I go from a meeting wrung dry."

She used the miracle of man "who lay sick with palsy" to illustrate her text of the four-square gospel. "The sick man is the sick world and the bed he lay upon is the word of God and the four cords with which his friend lifted him down through the roof into the presence of Christ are 'Salvation,' 'Baptism of the Holy Ghost,' 'Divine Healing' and 'The Second Coming of Christ.' "

The woman intrigued Texas Guinan — her full-throated contralto voice and excellent enunciation in quick speech. Texas remembered no actress who ever sounded more clearly the last letters or took advantage of vowels and diphthongs with greater effect. Mrs. McPherson's brown eyes flashed or were luminous with tears at will. Her marcelled hair was dressed to a peak above the long face and large, expressive mouth, and her white nurse's costume with a blue cape hung from the shoulders reflected the light.

Likening herself to the boy who brought the loaves and fishes with which Jesus fed the multitude, she prayed that she might be broken. "Jesus, do you remember — but of course you do — the miracle of the fishes? Break our wills, break us up so there'll be enough to go around. Break our hearts."

And the audience of thousands cried: "Amen."

Hymns followed, the first "Onward, Christian Soldiers," and in quick succession, several other standbys of the emotionalist theologian, backed by a brass band dominated by sharp trumpets and trombones.

"Most of those present seemed to have come to have their emotions worked upon, and they were," said the *Times*. "After the services Miss Guinan shook hands with the evangelist . . ."

Mrs. McPherson then went to the McAlpin Hotel, where she appeared at a dinner for executives of the *New York Graphic* before departing for stops at Syracuse and Rochester, thence to Florida and back to California.

Texas failed to attend the scheduled morning session with U.S. Commissioner Cotter "for fear of missing Mrs. McPherson's sermon," she said. Her attorney told the commissioner he had not thought her personal appearance would be necessary and gave the inclement weather as an excuse. The hearing was reset for February 24.

Texas was present. However, the case again was postponed until February 25, pending receipt of the government chemist's report that the pint of liquor seized in the raid was "synthetic Scotch, artificially colored and made from redistilled denatured alcohol."

On February 25 the charges against Hagen and Litwin were dismissed. Guinan, Edson, and Golden were bound over for trial and their bails continued.

Meanwhile, Judge Bondy approved a personal injunction making manager Edson liable for contempt of court for violating the previous temporary injunction against the 300 Club. At 5:00 in the afternoon, Captain Inglesby snapped a padlock which would interrupt Texas Guinan's career for six months.

The trial before Federal Judge Thomas D. Thacher on March 30 was a heated one. "I certainly did not order any waiter to serve liquor to any patron at the 300 Club," Texas testified. "Just before the holidays George Levy [club treasurer] gave orders that no more liquor was to be served." Mr. Levy, she said, owned the club. She had signed a contract with him in December 1925 to "put on the show" for a weekly salary of $1,000, and "extras" for any additional performance.

Levy testified that on December 15 he had given orders to every employee not to sell liquor at the club.

Captain Inglesby told of finding the December 22 injunction in a cuspidor. Attorney Edelstein submitted that such injunctions as Miss Guinan was accused of violating had been held illegal by the judge himself in previous test cases. Then the attorney dropped his bombshell. Edelstein introduced evidence to show that the bottle of whiskey allegedly purchased at the 300 Club had, in fact, been taken from prohibition headquarters at 1 Park Avenue and used by the prohibition agent to aid in establishing himself as a "good fellow."

Judge Thacher found that the government had failed to prove beyond a reasonable doubt that the defendants had participated in the sale of liquor on the premises, and ordered them freed.

Ethel Waters, the number-one black actress and hot and low-down cabaret singer who put herself on the discs with "Shake That Thing," would take over the 300 Club but soon had to close. It was reopened by Raymond Hitchcock, as Club Hitchy, but flopped again in the show business slump and decline in the nation's prosperity toward the end of the decade.

CHAPTER 8

Padlocks of 1927

Undeterred, Texas continued to frolic with her dancers and singers in other resorts. While her family visited old friends in Waco, she investigated possibilities in Philadelphia — and suffered a personal tragedy. Upon returning to New York, she found that her West Eighth Street flat had been flooded with water. The screams of a parrot for two hours had attracted neighbors who summoned a policeman. The policeman broke into the place and discovered that a pipe had burst on the second floor. Much of the memorabilia Texas had collected over the years was ruined. Damage to clothing, furniture, and tapestries amounted to $20,000.

In April, Duo Art Productions, Inc., with Edward A. Everett as president and Anton Scibilia and C. William Morganstern (connected with Mae West's recent production, *Sex*) as directors, sponsored a Broadway revue in which Texas was to receive $3,500 a week for her appearance. The chorus line was clothed in necklaces and belts of little U-shaped bars passed through the staples of hasps. The revue was appropriately titled *Padlocks of 1927*.

Padlocks opened at the Shubert Theater. It was no less ribald and gaudy than the proceedings in Guinan's night clubs. Though the talent was thin and its humor consisted largely of stale prohibition jokes, its imposing mistress of ceremonies carried the show.

Texas boasted in one song "the wail of the sucker is sweet to my ears," and as each of her singers delivered their solo numbers, she appealed to the audience: "Give the little girl a great big hand."

The production ran seventeen weeks — then into trouble. Scibilia and Morganstern withdrew their sponsorship and were replaced by two nontheatrical investors. For several days in September there were Broadway reports that the cast was in protest over back salaries. One night the curtain was held for fifteen minutes because of an altercation. On September 23, Texas announced that she was ending her engagement and that arbitration proceedings at the Actors' Equity Association headquarters had begun.

The arbitration board awarded her $26,000 — the difference between the salary promised by Duo Art Productions and the amount she had actually received. President Everett appealed on grounds that the hearing by the board was "informal and no sworn testimony was taken." On September 17, however, Texas had threatened to walk out of the show unless Everett signed an agreement to arbitrate her claim. The producer did so, and it was on the basis of this agreement that Supreme Court Justice Ford finally upheld the board's decision.

Texas won this suit, but lost another. Wynn Holcomb, an artist, of Jackson Heights, Queens, sued her for $1,450 allegedly due him for providing caricatures of forty stage and screen celebrities, among which was one of Texas herself, used to decorate the walls of a night club where she was entertaining. At the trial before City Court Justice Wendel and a jury, in May 1928, Holcomb testified that Miss Guinan had contracted for the series of pictures then failed to pay for them. Texas stated that she was only an employee of the club, had no financial interest in it, and had never "talked money" with Holcomb. "I will not pay what I do not owe!" she declared. The jury favored the artist and Justice Wendel ruled that she owed him $700 for his work.

Texas suffered another setback. When her application to open a night club in the Century Theater Building was denied by New York's licensing commissioner, she managed, with the help of friends, to take over a resort at 310 West Fifty-eighth Street, renamed Texas Guinan's Salon Royale. Early the morning of June 29, more than 160 local and visiting prohibition agents, led by Agent Thomas Shannon, working in squads of a half dozen men dressed in evening clothes, made surprise forays on the Salon Royale and seventeen other leading Broadway clubs and cabarets.

Every precaution had been taken to prevent news of the raids "leaking" about Broadway. The agents had been locked up in prohibition headquarters at 1 Park Avenue, with the telephones disconnected, and kept in ignorance of where they were to go until separated into squads and dispatched to the various destinations. "Between midnight and 3 o'clock," said the *Times*, "eleven clubs had been closed, the waiters, entertainers, orchestras and guests driven to the street and in many instances principals and employees arrested."

At the Summer Home, agents "tore out the furniture and fittings." Helen Morgan eluded them by "changing costumes with her cloakroom girl and quietly slipping out during the search." Texas Guinan "was not at her club . . . and persons associated with her in the business . . . said this was the first time any of her clubs had been raided while she was absent." It was rumored later that, despite the precautions taken to prevent a "leak," she had been "tipped off"; when the agents arrived, she was smuggled out of the place "in the hands of her subordinates."

Within an hour after the raiders left their headquarters, prisoners began to stream into the West Thirtieth Street and West Forty-seventh Street police stations — nearly 200 of them — where they were held until morning before transferred to the Federal Building and herded into the courtroom of U.S. Commissioner Cotter. A man from Butte, Montana, and another who said he was a lawyer from Ohio, maintained they were merely visitors at the club where arrested and had done nothing wrong to merit such treatment. Commissioner Cotter, however, "made no exceptions to the procedure of fixing bail at $1,000 in every case."

When several of the agents were identified with what was known as the "mop-up" squad in Washington, it was alleged that Assistant Attorney General Mabel Walker Willebrandt had personally planned the raids. Supposedly, the raids were connected with the adoption of a dry plank at the Republican National Convention at Kansas City on June 12 (at which Secretary of Commerce Herbert Hoover received the nomination for president and Senator Charles Curtis of Kansas for the vice-presidency) and were otherwise political in character. Prohibition Administrator Maurice Campbell refused to comment. In Washington, Prohibition Commissioner Doran was quoted as saying: "The particular places in New York visited last night have been under scrutiny for five or six weeks."

Nonetheless, the prohibition officials seemed irked that both Guinan and Helen Morgan had escaped.

Word soon reached the women that Prohibition Administrator Campbell had threatened to issue warrants if they did not "surrender voluntarily." Texas and Helen "trekked" down to his headquarters. Campbell wasn't in, and no one knew his whereabouts. Nor could any affidavits or accusations against them be found.

They proceeded to the United States attorney's office. Assistant U.S. Attorney Robert B. Watts received them in his superior's absence, but he, too, was at a loss finding papers drawn up against the pair. Finally, they reached the office of U.S. Commissioner Cotter and were informed they faced new charges of violating the Volstead Act. Texas declared the charges had no basis of fact and stemmed from the "venom" of Administrator Campbell. This Commissioner Cotter disregarded. He complimented the women for having given themselves up, then followed his same procedure in dealing with the numerous cases brought before him the morning previous — set bail at $1,000 each for further hearing July 19.

It seemed an appropriate moment for New York's Committee of Fourteen (organized in 1905 to investigate evidences of commercialized prostitution) to release its annual report on the social standards and morality of the city. In general, the report charged that conditions were the worst in twenty years; specifically, it attributed the increase to the development of night clubs and speakeasies.

The main body of the report, written by George E. Worthington, general secretary and counsel, stated in part:

> The speakeasy situation is as serious, if not more so, as the Raines-law hotel which called this committee into existence and, with the assistance of the Brewers Board of Trade, the bonding companies and the Police Department, was completely suppressed long before the Federal Prohibition Act was passed . . .
>
> Some speakeasy-clubs are cloaked with an apparent respectability likely to throw the unsophisticated off guard . . . They are attracting young men and young women, which the Raines-law hotel and the saloon with the back door never catered to . . . were not permitted to go to such lengths. This is a matter that the people of New York must

consider. The cooperation which previously existed with the brewers and bonding companies is impossible now. The police and the committee must face the problem without these important auxilaries.

Dr. James Pedersen, committee chairman, contributed an introduction in which he acknowledged the "important co-operation" of the American Social Hygiene Association and of the Bureau of Social Hygiene. The association was cited for "turning over to the committee its local investigative staff, with a fund for investigation purposes," and the bureau for a "special grant to finance a study of the part played by night clubs and speakeasies in making new victims."

The report listed 157 night clubs and speakeasies investigated in 1927, nearly eighty-five percent of which were "identified with commercial vice." Of 441 women observed in such places, sixty-six percent were "known to be of this character," and the remaining 150 "hostesses whom investigators did not question because the expense of repeated visits to obtain evidence was prohibitive."

Without mentioning names, Secretary Worthington zeroed in on women like Guinan and Helen Morgan:

> The speakeasy clubs are now too numerous to succeed without the added attraction of "hostesses" . . . The greatest demand appeared in the Fall of 1927 when agencies and some tabloids became bold enough to advertise for recruits . . . drawing not only local girls into this occupation, but also girls from various parts of the United States.
>
> The hostess of the speakeasy-club is the American counterpart of the Geisha girl. She is employed for the main purpose of increasing the sales of food, liquor and other drinks, and incidentally, provide esthetic social and sexual entertainment for the men customers. She is the successor of the old-time hustler who worked in bars on a commission basis and was divorced from the saloon business long before the Volstead Act went into effect.

New York's police commissioner received the committee's report July 9, and told newspapermen who ringed his desk that he did not intend to adopt any new policy of suppressing vice in the city. He asserted that action had been taken in every case that the committee had turned over to the police, where there was a possibility of sustaining the evidence. But he was unable to discuss the cases in detail due to the absence on vacation of Deputy Inspector Lewis J. Valentine, who was in charge of vice investigations. Asked if iniquity was as widespread in the city as pictured, he declared crisply: "It is not so."

Texas Guinan echoed the official police view after hurrying from the beach to meet reporters at her Greenwich Village apartment. She didn't know about speakeasies or the "lower strata of night clubs," but nothing "rough or tough" was ever permitted at a club where she presided.

"No, sir," she snapped. She sipped black coffee and threatened between swallows to launch a libel action.

"Come up to the club tonight," she said, "and meet the mothers of the kids in my place. They call for them every night. I won't stand for any freshness . . . I've put out some of the best people in New York just because they forgot themselves. I stop the music and out they go.

"This report calls hostesses prostitutes. That is a plain outrage and in the country where I come from they have to eat words like that.

"I'll give $100,000 to anybody who can prove that I was ever associated with anything off color in my life . . . I challenge the authors of that report to a debate and I'll pay them plenty for their time."

Texas asked Secretary Worthington for an interview at his office to discuss conditions at the Salon Royale. Worthington agreed. He set the time at 9:30 A.M., July 10, but canceled the meeting after he learned that "Miss Guinan's press agent had sent word to all the newspapers, asking them to send reporters to attend." The committee, he stated, did not wish to "advance any private publicity device."

Secretary Worthington softened his view. He admitted that some of the night clubs were "respectable," but "refused to name the six which had been given a clean bill of health in the committee report." He also acknowledged the increase in police activity: "They cannot exercise the same surveillance over the speakeasies that they did over saloons, with the growth of such places so great, but if they continue their present spurt there will be marked decreases in speakeasies within six months . . . If there was some way of putting the speakeasies out of commission, this problem of commercialized vice would cease to exist as far as the Committee of Fourteen is concerned."

The government did its part. On July 30 a federal grand jury indicted 108 persons for conspiracy and maintenance of a nuisance for alleged roles in the operation of the eighteen resorts raided on June 29. Eighteen true bills were handed Federal Judge Frank T. Coleman, and entered to await their turn on the trial calendar. Heading the list were Helen Morgan's Summer Home and the Salon Royale.

Heretofore, the conspiracy charge had been confined almost entirely to rum rings, distillery operations, and thefts from liquor warehouses. It now included the illegal operation of night clubs and speakeasies with the aid of others who might be merely employees, and was added to the temporary padlock as a weapon on the prohibition enforcement battleground. Maintenance of a nuisance carried a maximum penalty of one year imprisonment and a $1,000 fine. Conspiracy was punishable by a maximum of two years in prison and a fine of $10,000. Assistant U.S. attorneys Arthur H. Schwartz and Robert B. Watts, who presented the evidence to the grand jury, stated that every effort had been made to "use all the teeth in the law," and that the government was proceeding on the theory that "each night club is a separate conspiracy."

Texas Guinan publicity photo, Night Life in New York *(Paramount, 1925), in which she appeared in person, and cast Rod LaRocque, Ernest Torrence, Dorothy Gish, Helen Lee Worthing, and George Hackethorne.*

Texas Guinan, New York night club queen (ca. 1927).

Helen Morgan — Guinan's one rival in business and personality — operated her Summer Home club on West Fifty-second Street.

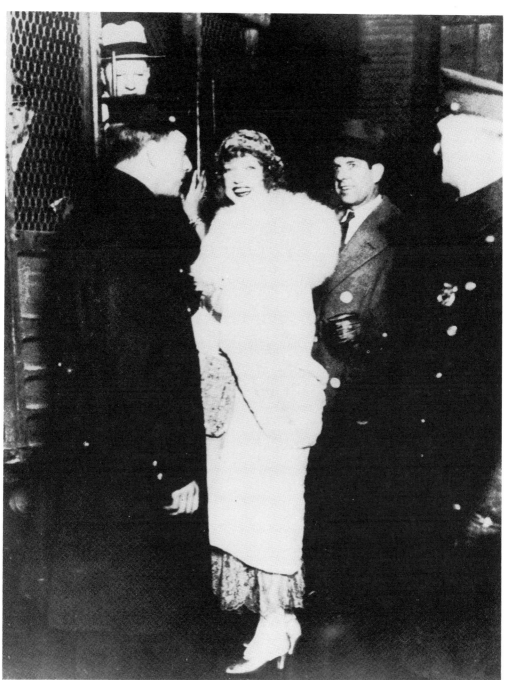

Texas Guinan flashes cameraman a smile as she is escorted to a paddy wagon follow-ing dry raid on the 300 Club. She was held in a cell for nine hours — the only time she ever spent in jail.

TEXAS GUINAN CLUB SHUT FOR 10 MONTHS

Helen Morgan Place Is Also Closed and Both Face Personal Injunctions.

HEARING SET FOR MONDAY

European Club and Village Bar Rail Among Others Which Are Padlocked.

Texas Guinan, recently found not guilty of maintaining a nuisance at the Salon Royal, and Helen Morgan, acquitted of a similar charge involving Helen Morgan's Summer Home, must come into court again on Monday as a result of the issuance yesterday of padlock decrees against these two night clubs.

Despite the decisions of the two Federal trial juries which heard the evidence in the two "nuisance" cases, Miss Guinan and Miss Morgan must satisfy Federal Judge Alfred C. Coxe Jr. as to whether they have actually violated the Volstead act in any manner and whether they should be "enjoined forever" against vio-

TEXAS GUINAN JAILED IN DRY RAID ON CLUB

Hostess and Three Employes Are Locked Up Charged With Prohibition Law Violation.

HAD BEEN RAIDED BEFORE

And She Is Also Charged With Contempt of Court—No Bail Without Federal Court Order.

"Texas" Guinan, one of Broadway's best known night club hostesses, and three of her "300 Club" employes at 151 West Fifty-fourth Street, were arrested and locked up in the West Forty-seventh Street Station early today after a dozen Federal prohibition agents had raided the club. It is alleged that three of the agents had spent many hours in the club last night and early today making merry and openly buying liquor.

The raid was made a little before 3 o'clock this morning, the night club curfew hour, when the club was

Texas Guinan in New York Times *headlines during dry raids of 1927–1928.*

Tex Guinan Take Drink? No! Sell Booze? Never!

Nasty Stuff Brought Into Her Club, But What Can a Girl Do?

NEW YORK, April 10—(AP)—Texas Guinan, who started her 20-year stage carreer as a vaudeville performer and star in the early movie westerns and now is a night club hostess with a $1,000 a week guarantee, took the witness stand Wednesday to testify that if the Salon Royale is a nuisance it is none of her doing.

Giving the crowd in the federal courtroom, where she is on trial, the same broad smile with which she is accustomed to shout, "Hello, Sucker," to the Salon Royale's patrons, Miss Guinan told of her part in the city's night life, intermittently sniffing at a bottle of perfumed salts.

"Have you ever sold any liquor in the Salon Royale?" her lawyer asked.

"I have never sold liquor in my entire life," she said.

"Did you ever take a drink?"

"I have never had a drink in my entire life."

"Did you know that liquor was sold there?"

"I did not."

"Did you ever see any liquor there?"

"Well, I saw what looked like liquor. People brought suitcases of liquor in and served it themselves."

Before the government rested late Wednesday three prohibition agents testified to having bought champagne and whisky in the night club, although not from the hostess herself.

The last evidence offered by the prosecution had to do with the Guinan contract with the Salon Royale and the books of the night club. The contract showed that she was paid half of the net profits from all sources, with a guarantee of $1,000 a week.

Miss Guinan's contention was that she was employed purely as an artist and was not responsible for any wrongdoing that may have been done in the place by others.

Texas Guinan in her starring role as "Tex Malone," in Queen of the Night Clubs, *a Vitaphone all-talking picture written especially for her and produced by Warner Brothers, 1929.*

Texas Guinan appeared in person in Florenz Ziegfeld's musical-revue drama titled Glorifying the American Girl, *featuring Mary Eaton (Paramount, 1929).*

Scene from Glorifying the American Girl *(Paramount, 1929)*.

TEXAS GUINAN CLUB SCENE OF SHOOTING

Ex-Business Associate, Trying to Collect Rent for Green Mill in Chicago, Gets Bullets.

HER MANAGER IS HELD

Miss Guinan Talks On, Band Plays as Lead Flies—She "Doesn't Know a Thing About It."

Special to The New York Times.

CHICAGO, March 23.—Three shots closed Texas Guinan's show at the Green Mill at 4 o'clock this morning when Leon Sweitzer, once part owner of the café, and at present the owner of the Little Club, ran down a stairway from a balcony pursued by two men firing at him and whom he said were Harry G. Voiler, manager for Miss Guinan, and Arthur Reed, bodyguard for Voiler.

Sweitzer, a former policeman and a nephew of County Clerk Robert H. Sweitzer, was shot in the arm and leg and a third bullet struck a rib and was deflected. He probably

BAR TEXAS GUINAN FROM FRENCH VISIT

Officials Prohibit Night Club Job as Her "Gang" Fumes in Havre Hotel.

SCANT ATTIRE STIRS SHIP

Clergymen Reported Shocked on Crossing—Party Held Up Because of Wrong Papers.

Special Cable to The New York Times.

PARIS, May 29.—No one in Europe wants Texas Guinan, it seems, so she and "her gang" were waiting at Havre tonight, with no place to go.

When Miss Guinan was notified aboard the liner Paris that she couldn't land in England, she said she didn't care and would go to Paris. But when the liner arrived at Havre today French special police went aboard and, after examining passports, declared that the "Guinan gang" could not remain in France.

Shooting in Green Mill Club, Chicago, closes Texas Guinan show, March 1930.

Texas Guinan show barred from entering England and France (May–June 1931).

Texas Guinan on horse Pieface, in Labor Day parade at Pasadena, California, 1933.

Guinan's last film appearance. Texas Guinan (Tex Kaley) romances Hugh O'Con-
nell (Chuck Haskins) while Blossom Seely (Sybil Smith) looks on, in scene from
Broadway Thru A Keyhole *(20th Century production, 1933).*

10,000 VIEW BODY OF TEXAS GUINAN

Crowd Files Past Bier of Actress Brought Here From Vancouver for Burial.

NOTABLES SEND FLOWERS

Funeral Will Be Held Today, With Burial in the Gate of Heaven Cemetery.

Texas Guinan came back yesterday to Broadway.

The body of the actress and night club entertainer was taken to the Campbell Funeral Church, Broadway, between Sixty-sixth and Sixty-seventh Streets, and there placed in the room where Rudolph Valentino's body was viewed by a throng of 75,000.

There was no such gathering for Miss Guinan, but there was a crowd, which during the afternoon amounted to something like 10,000 to 12,000 persons. By nightfall the throng had dwindled away.

Beginning at noon, people filed through the funeral church in a single line, at a rate of thirty a minute. They entered through the

Thousands viewed the body of Texas Guinan in New York, November 12, following her death at Vancouver, British Columbia, November 5, 1933.

Phyllis Diller (on stage) impersonates Texas Guinan, in Splendor in the Grass *(Warner Brothers, 1961).*

Betty Hutton played Texas Guinan in Incendiary Blonde *(Paramount Pictures, 1945).*

Principal cast of Lady For A Day *(Columbia Pictures, 1933). From left: Jean Parker, Guy Kibbe, May Robson, Warren William, and Glenda Farrell, in her Guinan role as "Missouri Martin."*

Barbara Nichols impersonates Texas Guinan in The George Raft Story *(Allied Artists, 1961)*.

CHAPTER 9

Queen of the Night Clubs

The grand jury indictments voided the necessity for hearings on defendants arraigned and bonded in U.S. Commissioner Cotter's court. On August 6 the dingy corridors of the Federal Building echoed the tramp and scrape of feet as some 200 alleged offenders gathered for argument or final disposition, accompanied by attorneys, friends, bondsmen, and scores of merely curious. While interest centered on the more than 100 indicted for conspiracy and maintaining nuisances, the small fry shared the stage. Ninety-five, hoping for leniency, pleaded guilty to liquor violations and were fined in amounts of $10 to $250 each. For the others who elected to stand trial, new bails were fixed and in some cases increased.

Several alleged conspirators failed to appear, either in person or through counsel. Bench warrants were ordered for their arrests. The absentees included Helen Morgan. Later, she appeared with her attorney and "the bench warrant was held up." She pleaded not guilty to maintenance of a nuisance and made bail, with the announcement that she was quitting the booze battle because of the wear and tear on her nerves — and the high costs of her gowns.

Texas Guinan arrived for court early, wearing a black ensemble, a broad smile, and an air of bored intolerance. She had received no official notice, she declared, but had "called at the Federal Building because of newspaper reports that she had been indicted." Wisecracking, as always, she wanted to know if it was an "invitation affair." Nevertheless, she was accompanied by her attorney, Walter Sollinger, and the indicted alleged owners of the Salon Royale, John M. and Ernest Johnnidis.

She had nothing to say when arraigned for maintenance of a nuisance, except that she was "just a working girl who received a cut of the club's receipts." Assistant U.S. Attorney James H. Terry asked that a bail for each of the Salon Royale trio be fixed at $2,500. Texas Guinan's smile returned when Federal Judge Isaac M. Meekins decided that $1,000 would be sufficient.

Told afterwards by a reporter that Helen Morgan was retiring from the night club "racket," and asked if she had thought of doing likewise, Texas replied: "Honey, I'm no quitter."

On August 14, Sollinger attempted to interest veteran trial lawyer Clarence S. Darrow in the Guinan hassle. Darrow was famed mostly for saving from execution wealthy Chicago youths Nathan Leopold and Richard Loeb for the kidnap-murder of Robert Franks, in 1924, and his 1925 encounter with William Jennings Bryan in the Scopes evolution trial in Tennessee. He was stopping at the Belmont Hotel, en route to New England on vacation.

After a brief conference with Sollinger, Darrow declined. "I'm writing some articles," he said. "I will visit Cold Harbor, Massachusetts, Boston and possibly go to the White Mountains before returning to Chicago." His schedule precluded delving into the merits of the case.

Her case pending, Texas continued to perform at the Salon Royale, the indisputable "queen" of New York's nightlife. Or so thought some in the motion picture industry. In September she reported to Hollywood on contract with Warner Brothers to star as "Tex Malone" in a Vitaphone all-talking picture, written especially for her by Addison Burkhart and Murray Roth, directed by Bryan Foy, and titled *Queen of the Night Clubs*.

Her arrival in Los Angeles evoked official disapproval and unfavorable comment. Many saw fit to snub her, either in resentment to her reentering motion pictures or because they had their own night club hostesses to admire. A 1,000-plate dinner to be held in her honor at the Breakfast Club's pavillion, scene of many gatherings in honor of distinguished visitors, was canceled after Mayor

George Cryer himself refused to take part in the welcoming ceremonies.

It was great publicity for her picture. Warner Brothers moved
into high gear. The cast included such lights as John and William
Davidson, Lila Lee, Arthur Housman, Eddie Foy, Jr., Jack Nor-
worth, George Raft, Jimmie Phillips, Lee Shumway, James T.
Mack, Agnes Traney, Charlotte Merriam, and Joseph Depew, with
the song: "It's Tough To Be a Hostess on Broadway."

The picture was released in late February 1929 and opened at
the Mark Strand Theater in New York in March. It presented a
new and svelte Miss Guinan, with hair bleached almost blonde,
and considerably more attractive than when she rode the cinema
range — to the credit of both Texas and Warner Brothers' makeup
man. Some critics, however, observed that she was no more of an
actress than she had been a decade earlier. A review in the *Times* of
March 18 is worthy of note:

> The Vitaphone production is somewhat of a thriller,
> with a murder or so, frowning plotters, a silly hoofer and a
> none-too-gifted young woman who, nevertheless, appears to
> be worth her weight in gold as an entertainer in a night
> club.
>
> Miss Guinan's voice is more powerful than melodious.
> It is the voice that is accustomed to ordering guests to buy
> and buy and give little girls a hand. Following the murder,
> which must happen in every night club on the screen, Miss
> Guinan . . . admits on the witness stand that she knows
> more about Scotch than English, a joke that was thought to
> have sunk into oblivion . . .
>
> Her success as a night club hostess who is favored by
> those who patronize these nocturnal resorts . . . causes her
> rivals to plot her downfall, especially Don Holland [John
> Davidson] who supplies the boodle.
>
> In at least one incident . . . the police are depicted as
> being exceptionally callous regarding murders. They order
> two stretchers over the telephone, with about the same cool-
> ness a butter and egg man might order mineral water in a
> Texas Guinan club . . .
>
> Lila Lee impersonates Bee Walters, the girl who makes
> a strong impression upon the night club crowds. Eddie
> Parr, the silly young hoofer, is fairly well acted by Eddie
> Foy, Jr. John Davidson appears to be thinking too much of

his voice and not enough of his gestures and expressions in playing Don Holland . . .

The scenes in the courtroom are both well filmed and competently acted. Those filling the roles of the lawyers do their work naturally . . .

The denouement . . . is by no means as imaginative as one anticipates. The author appears to have been floundering around to find a way out and ended his yarn the best he could. And this best is amateurishly forced.

Queen of the Night Clubs enjoyed a modest success in the movie houses, while back at the Salon Royale, Texas still packed them in. When her case came to trial on April 10, she needed no Clarence Darrow for defense.

Texas's new counsel, attorney Maxwell E. Lopin, put her on the stand to testify that "if the Salon Royale is a nuisance it was none of my doing." Giving the crowd in the courtroom the same broad smile with which she was accustomed to shout "Hello, sucker," she described her role in New York's nightlife as "only a paid entertainer," as she had successfully maintained so many times in the past.

"Have you ever sold any liquor in the Salon Royale?" her attorney asked.

"I have never sold liquor in my entire life," she said.

"Did you ever take a drink?"

"I have never had a drink in my entire life."

"Did you know that liquor was sold there?"

"I did not."

"Did you ever see any liquor there?"

"Well, I saw what looked like liquor. People brought it in and served it themselves."

Three prohibition agents testified to having bought champagne and whiskey in the club, but not from the hostess. Guinan's contract and the night club's books were offered in evidence to show that she received a guarantee of $1,000 a week and half of the net profits from all sources. Again the government failed to show that she was not employed solely as an artist or was responsible for any wrongdoing by others.

Texas was acquitted.

Helen Morgan went on trial April 17 before Federal Judge Edwin S. Thomas and "a jury of middle-aged and elderly men, of whom four were listed as 'retired,' two others as having 'no occupations' and one of whom admitted a prejudice against prohibition enforcement methods."

Through the testimony of two prohibition agents, the government unfolded a tale of alleged "whoopee-making" by Miss Morgan, in which numerous drinks of brandy were served as she sat upon the bar, sang "Ol' Man River" from Florenz Ziegfeld's acclaimed Broadway production, *Show Boat,* and tossed dollar bills at the black dancers.

Contrary to guilty pleas of the six employees under the same indictment, Miss Morgan's attorney showed that the half-dozen pints of brandy in question had been brought to her place by an outside party — two pints of which the agents themselves had purchased at $15 each. An extended cross-examination developed no new evidence.

Miss Morgan, silent and self-effacing throughout the proceedings (in striking contrast to Texas Guinan), smiled faintly as she took the stand and stated that the agents had "laid a trap" to effect her arrest.

The jury found her not guilty.

Despite their acquittals by two federal trial juries, both Guinan and Morgan were summoned before Federal Judge Alfred C. Coxe, Jr., to show why they should not be enjoined against "flouting the prohibition statutes in any manner whatsoever." M. M. Edelstein, attorney for the Salon Royale, and J. Arthur Adler, of Helen Morgan's Summer Home, consented to the issuance of padlock decrees without trial. Whereupon Judge Coxe ordered the resorts closed and that personal injunctions be served upon all managers and waiters of both establishments.

As promised, Helen Morgan gave up night club life. Texas Guinan jumped back into the fire.

CHAPTER 10

Glorifying the American Girl

A movement was on to repeal the Eighteenth Amendment. In March of 1929, Herbert Hoover had taken the oath of office as the thirty-first president of the United States after easily defeating New York's dynamic politician and fourth-term governor, Alfred E. Smith, whose Catholic religion and "wet" stand on the prohibition issue had proved embarrassing to the Democratic Party.

Earlier, Assistant Secretary of the Treasury Lincoln C. Andrews, in charge of the Prohibition Bureau, testified before the Senate Judiciary Committee to the staggering difficulties of enforcing the provisions of the Volstead Act with only 3,374 agents and an annual budget of $8 million. Some 900 agents had been dismissed due to lack of funds and a variety of prohibition-related offenses. The bureau, with whatever aid it could muster from state and local authorities, had caught one-twentieth of the liquor smuggling on 18,000 miles of coastline (calculated at between five and ten million gallons a year) and seized more than 170,000 stills (about one-tenth of the stills in existence). Twenty million otherwise respectable citizens concocted homebrew, wines, or "bathtub gins," and bootleggers were earning an estimated $4 million annually.

In the large cities across the country, gangsters had built underworld empires based on the smuggling, manufacture, and distribution of liquor, extending into slot machines and labor unions, and guarded by armies of gunmen. Between 1920 and 1927, more than 250 gangsters had been killed in Chicago warfare alone. It was noted that 190 persons had died as a direct result of enforcing the prohibition law, fifty-five of whom were government agents. Assistant Secretary Lincoln asked that $30 million be budgeted to strengthen all prohibition enforcement agencies.

Despite the expense and difficulties, temperance groups maintained that the nation was generally better off under prohibition. On the contrary, the Bar Association of New York City declared itself against the Volstead Act, and President Hoover, speaking before the Associated Press at New York in April 1929, recognized that prohibition-related crime was creating a series of social and political problems. In May he appointed a Law Observance and Enforcement Commission headed by former Attorney General George W. Wickersham to conduct a survey to serve as a basis for formulating public policy on the Eighteenth Amendment. It became clearly evident that the enforcement of the amendment had broken down when the government quashed a series of conspiracy indictments, saying it was almost impossible to find a jury that would convict night club operators who sold illegal liquor.

Even before her acquittal, Texas Guinan, with brother Tommy and her associate Hyman Edson, took over the Club Intime, a cabaret tenant of the Hotel Harding at 203–211 West Fifty-fourth Street. Her reign there was of short duration. On April 4, New York's new police commissioner, Grover Whalen, estimated that there were 32,000 speakeasies in the city, tabbed them as the cause of the great increase in crime, and asserted that, despite judges who were "soft" on criminals and "hard" on police methods, prohibition laws and building ordinances would be enforced. Texas not only underestimated the police commissioner's determination, but had the Intime proprietors partition the leased portion of the hotel as a separate restaurant, which required a certificate of occupancy.

A notice from the Department of Licenses sent to Andrew J. Kerwin, president of the West Side Hotel Corporation and owner of the Harding, was delivered to the firm of Sladen and Ginsberg, lessee of the hotel. The firm contended that, since the Club Intime occupied quarters in the Harding, it was a part of the hotel and should be exempted. License Commissioner William F. Quigley held otherwise. A summons and search warrant was issued by the West Side Court.

Shortly after midnight, April 17, as Texas was about to begin her show, Detective Anthony Laroussee handed the assistant manager the summons, while a squad of plainclothes patrolmen led by Lt. Patrick Kenneally invaded the establishment. They immediately arrested six employees (including the Chinese chef) for handling food without Health Department permits. Sixty patrons who had pushed back their chairs and were waiting expectantly for the performers to appear were told there would be no show. A uniformed patrolman was left on guard to prevent the show from proceeding until the matter could be litigated.

In turn, Texas and attorney Maxwell Lopin called on Supreme Court Justice Henry L. Sherman and instituted injunction proceedings against Commissioner of Licenses Quigley; Police Commissioner Whalen; Police Inspector Joseph P. Loonan, commanding the Third Division, which included the Broadway Forties; and Capt. Louis F. Dittman of the West Forty-seventh Station, where the prisoners had been taken for bail. The order, signed and served that afternoon, directed the officials to appear at 10:00 A.M., April 18, before Supreme Court Justice Edward P. Gavegan "to show cause why they should not be temporarily restrained from interfering with the operation of the Club Intime."

The order, if successfully argued, would prevent the police from interfering with the club until a permanent injunction or other process cleared it from Local Law No. 12. "This," Lopin told Texas, "may take several months."

Their hopes were shaken by two outside attacks. President Kerwin, who was "absolutely opposed" to the club as a tenant of the Harding, sought an order restraining the club from making alterations. Lopin pointed out that there had been three lessees of the hotel in succession, and therefore, Kerwin could not take action. Mrs. Tillie Landauer had leased the hotel in 1923 and operated it until December 1926, when she subleased it to Sladen and Ginsberg. Mrs. Landauer revealed that she had dispossessed Sladen and Ginsberg for nonpayment of rent in February, and wishing to investigate carefully before giving another lease, had refused to accept rent from or recognize the Club Intime as a tenant. She sided with Kerwin, stating that the club "would probably be put out of its present quarters if the things they have been accused of doing are true." Her attorney, Herman Wiesenthal, declared: "We can put them out, because we have dispossessed their landlords."

On April 18 the West Side Court adjourned the hearings on the six club employees "after they displayed what they claimed were permits to handle food." Meanwhile, Assistant Corporation Counsel Thomas W. A. Crowe, representing commissioners Whalen and Quigley, strongly opposed granting of the injunction in Justice Gavegan's court: "The injunction is sought not by the owner of the Hotel Harding, but by the plaintiff, a lessee and separate entity." Justice Gavegan ruled: "It is clear, indeed conceded, that the plaintiff operates a cabaret on the premises not licensed for the purpose in the manner prescribed by law. Such operation constitutes a misdemeanor under Section 11 of Local Law 12. A court of equity will therefore not enjoin the police in their efforts to prevent a continuation of such offense."

Two days later, attorney Wiesenthal asked Municipal Court Justice Thomas E. Murray for an eviction order, alleging the club was not only operating without a certificate of occupancy but had made certain alterations in its quarters without permission of the legal landlord, Mrs. Landauer. Justice Murray signed the order.

On April 26, City Marshal Michael J. Kennedy, Jr., appeared at the Club Intime. Tommy Guinan and Hyman Edson were present. Asked the nature of his visit, Kennedy replied: "I am probably the last sucker to step in here . . . I am going to give the little girl a great big hand." The marshal and his assistants removed all the furnishings and deposited them on the sidewalk. The draperies of the club were sent to a cleaning establishment. The rest of the paraphernalia was moved to the Chelsea Storage Warehouse on West Twenty-sixth Street.

Texas moved her troupe from the Broadway Forties to a Long Island roadhouse at Valley Stream. In July she turned down an offer from the Radio-Keith-Orpheum circuit to headline a new vaudeville bill opening at the Palace, because she found it impossible for her floor show to double between the roadhouse and the Broadway music hall. Later, when the Paramount Famous Lasky Corporation invited her to appear in person in a musical revue-drama supervised by Florenz Ziegfeld, titled *Glorifying the American Girl*, Texas accepted.

American Girl, released December 7, 1929, featured the Ziegfeld stage beauty Mary Eaton, loving, dancing, singing "There Must

Be Somebody." Basically a routine romance of a local girl who makes good on Broadway and rejects her man for the sake of stardom, the story was ditched at her debut for a lavish, breathtaking spectacle, which the audience really came to see. Many celebrities were introduced, beginning with Rudy Vallee crooning his signature song "I'm Just a Vagabond Lover," followed by Helen Morgan in a blues rendition of "What Wouldn't I Do For That Man" and Eddie Cantor doing his "Cheap Charlie" skit. Also "in person" were Mr. and Mrs. Ziegfeld, Adolph Zukor, banker Otto Kahn, Mayor and Mrs. Jimmy Walker, writer Ring Lardner, Noah Beery, Johnny Weismuller, and Texas Guinan. Mary Eaton reappeared as the premiere danseuse, and was a sensation.

Though a success, *American Girl* did little to bolster the lagging business along the Great White Way. America faced an uncertain future. The nation's postwar prosperity, sustained by residential construction, auto output, purchases of consumers' durable goods and new investment in producers' durable goods, had begun its decline in 1927. The increasing unemployment rate and great decrease in construction during 1928 should have been a warning. The boom continued, however, fed almost entirely by unprecedented securities speculation. On October 23–28, 1929, stock prices crashed spectacularly. Millions of shares changed hands and billions of dollars in value were lost. Investors jammed Wall Street, their fortunes wiped out. Economists, bankers, and politicians groped for an explanation to this overt inception of the Great Depression.

The big spenders who frequented Guinan's roadhouse at Valley Stream all but vanished. In mid-December, she took her troupe to Chicago. Harry G. Voiler managed the Green Mill cabaret in the Summerdale district. He held a four-month lease from Leon Sweitzer, a former policeman who also owned a night spot called the Little Club. Voiler booked the Guinan show to capture the trade for Christmas and New Year's.

Patrons of the Green Mill were not the big spenders Texas had anticipated. Her cut of the net receipts was less than at Valley Stream, and there was trouble. Miss Lorraine Hayes, one of her top dancers, was dismissed from the show after an altercation with Kitty O'Reilly and Dottie Wahl on the floor of the cabaret. Miss Hayes gained the sympathy of Solly Marks, a bodyguard for Sweitzer, and became a source of annoyance at the Green Mill.

Texas decided to leave Chicago after a gala farewell party that was scheduled for Saturday night, March 29, 1930.

Sweitzer insisted that his contract calling for rent until May 1 must be fulfilled. But Voiler told Texas that he intended to pay nothing after March 29. An eavesdropping Miss Hayes conveyed the information to Solly Marks, who relayed it to Sweitzer.

At 4:00 on the morning of March 23, with the Guinan show in full clamor, Sweitzer drove up to the Green Mill. He left Marks and Miss Hayes in the car and went inside to talk to Voiler. Voiler's bodyguard, Arthur Reed, escorted Sweitzer to Voiler's office at the head of the stairway leading to the balcony. What transpired there is conjecture.

Three shots rang out. Sweitzer ran down the stairs, pursued by Voiler and Reed, then dashed past the crowd and fell in the lobby. He had been hit in the arm and leg. A third bullet had struck a rib and deflected. The band kept playing and Texas continued her wisecracking and cheerleading while police rushed in and seized Voiler and Reed. Sweitzer was rushed to a hospital, where physicians said he would recover.

Texas, in evening dress, her wrists and neck banded with pearls and a white ermine wrap over her shoulders, went to the Summerdale police station and declared that she knew nothing about the affair, nor did her patrons. The shooting had "occurred upstairs and the rest of the excitement came in the lobby out of sight of the boys and girls who were whooping it up."

Voiler and Reed claimed that Sweitzer entered the office, threatening to seize the money in the cash register. At the hospital Sweitzer told Assistant State's Attorney Marovitz an argument over rent led to the attack on him. The police informed Guinan that Voiler was an ex-convict, having been sentenced to a fifteen- to thirty-year term in the Jackson, Michigan, penitentiary in 1918 for robbery; that his bodyguard Reed had served two prison terms, and had been released from a California penitentiary two days before Voiler employed him.

Texas didn't tarry. She canceled the farewell party, hied her girls back to New York, and reopened her old 300 Club at 151 West Fifty-fourth Street, now named the Argonaut. Immediately she became involved in the storm of protests against the Mastick law recently passed by the state legislature and signed by New York's new governor, Franklin D. Roosevelt.

The Mastick law limited the hours of overtime work for women in industry. Texas was invited to voice her opinion at a mass meeting held in Town Hall, under the auspices of the National Woman's Party, on May 18.

Mrs. Edith Houghton Hooker of Maryland, member of the National Council of the Woman's Party, presided. She opened by explaining that the law prohibited women working a minute overtime under the forty-eight-hour week, unless their hours were so arranged to give them a weekly half-holiday. "With the holiday, we may work only seventy-eight hours overtime a year," she said.

Jeannette Cortez, manager of a candy store and restaurant and a member of the Industrial Council of the Woman's Party, pointed to the "inconsistency" of the law which allowed her to work only forty-eight hours a week while standing behind the candy counter, but permitted her to work fifty-four hours a week as manager of the restaurant.

Mrs. Mary A. Murray, a railroad employee and chairwoman of the Industrial Council, followed with a denunciation of labor unions and welfare organizations which had encouraged the Mastick law as legislation to foster the welfare of women in industry.

"Actually, it is nothing more than a means of securing jobs for men against female competition," she declared. "Let the issue in the forthcoming State campaign be the demand for social equality . . . Labor unions get what they want through politics. They threaten with votes. Why shouldn't we?"

Gail Laughlin, member of the Maine state legislature and vice-president of the Woman's Party; Nina Broderick Price, president of the Zonta Club of New York; and Frances G. Roberts, treasurer of the Industrial Council, also advised making equality in industry a political issue.

So did Texas Guinan. "Why, we could swamp the politicians who refused to assist us, if we combined our vote in the proper way!" She agreed that the intent of the Mastick law was to protect men in industry, and urged that a "test case" be made of its constitutionality.

There is no record that Texas pursued the matter. Her appearance at the mass meeting was good publicity for the Woman's Party — and the Argonaut. She considered herself a "pawn" in prohibition politics and "struggled" to keep her girls working and out of the clutches of police and dry agents.

Prohibition was taking a back seat to unemployment as the chief national concern. Though most government leaders insisted that economic conditions were basically sound, industrial production of every type dropped steadily and businessmen retrenched during 1930. In October, President Hoover acknowledged publicly that unemployment stood at 4,500,000 in the nation's population of plus 123,000,000.

The Agricultural Marketing Bill of 1929 had established a Federal Farm Relief Board to assist farmers in setting up cooperative organizations but held no provision for subsidizing the sale of surplus commodities on the world market, as the majority of the Senate desired. Ignoring the objections of economists, the president had signed the Hawley-Smoot Tariff Act, raising import duties on hundreds of goods to record levels, which he contended would aid the hard-pressed farmer. He advocated a decentralized work relief policy that called for federal leadership of a national effort by agencies operating on a self-help basis in state and local communities, but he refused to concede that the government should provide direct assistance to the needy, as suggested by Senator Robert M. LaFollette, Jr., of Wisconsin, Governor Roosevelt, and others. Toward year's end, with the number of unemployed estimated at 7,000,000, the president asked Congress to authorize an expenditure of between $100 million and $150 million for waterway, harbor, flood control, public building, highway and airway improvement to stimulate the economy. Congress promptly approved $116 million.

Wages "held steady" as President Hoover attempted to convince the business community that a decrease would aggravate the nation's problems.

Patronage at the Broadway Forties night clubs and speakeasies also held steady. As Detective William McDonald of the Third Division stated to the *Times,* "customers are leaving these clubs so drunk that they are easy prey to thieves, unscrupulous taxi drivers and gangsters."

Shortly after 4:00 A.M., October 29, McDonald and his partner, Rudolph Serrett, entered the Argonaut and "saw couples drinking." A party of several "arrived with their bottles for a birthday breakfast and were promptly served with a nice green tub of ice." The detectives raided the club "while gayety was at its height and Miss Guinan was urging 200 guests to 'give her little girls a big hand.' " They seized "five bottles partly filled" with ginger ale and champagne, and arrested the head waiter, Bernardi Tann, and the club's secretary-treasurer, Bernard Altman. Tann and Altman were "arraigned before U.S. Commissioner Cotter for maintenance of a nuisance and possession and held in bail of $1,000 each." The detectives also alleged that an indecent dance had been staged at the club and "urged State authorities to take action for violation of the statute prohibiting such performances." In addition, Altman was charged in Magistrate Stanley Renaud's West Side Court with "conducting a cabaret without a license," and the Argonaut manager, Henry Kahn, was summoned for a padlock hearing.

Guinan and attorney Maxwell Lopin were present at each event. Lopin secured the release of Tann and Altman, and their hearing was set for November 10. Magistrate Renaud fined Altman $50, which Altman paid in protest.

Texas announced to the press that "about 150 persons depend upon my club for a livelihood . . . seventy-five entertainers and waiters and as many taxi drivers." If the detectives were successful in prosecuting the nuisance charge and the government padlocked the Argonaut, she said, "These dependents will be forced out of work, and this will complicate the city's unemployment problem." In deference to Miss Guinan's views, Lopin said he would apply to the licensing commissioner for a temporary permit.

This proved unnecessary. Manager Kahn, at his hearing on November 10, showed that the Argonaut had been organized as a "private corporation," and as such, was exempt from the cabaret licensing requirements. Magistrate Renaud dismissed the summons.

Meanwhile, Commissioner Cotter heard the testimony of detectives McDonald and Serrett. Cotter ruled: "Set-ups, including a tub of cracked ice for ginger ale and champagne, are not sufficient to hold defendants [Tann and Altman] for district court trial."

Police Commissioner Whalen, not to be discouraged, told the *Times:* "A drive to clean up New York night clubs will be begun."

CHAPTER 11

Too Hot for Paris

Texas continued to perform at the Argonaut, but her profits dwindled. Patrons had less to spend on night club revels. On December 11, 1930, the Bank of the United States in New York City failed in the largest bank collapse in the nation's history, affecting nearly 400,000 depositors. On Christmas Eve the Chelsea Bank and Trust Company, with six offices in the New York area, was forced to close by a run which started a day earlier.

The panic increased as the nation moved into 1931. More than 800 banks across the country failed in one two-month period. U.S. Steel and other large companies cut wages for hundreds of thousands of employees, and the number without jobs grew until private charity was unable to cope with the situation. Governor Roosevelt set up the Temporary Relief Administration for New York, with $20 million to be distributed through local governments. Other states adopted similar plans. On the national level, President Hoover appointed the President's Organization on Unemployment Relief to assist private charity to raise money. He also asked Congress to establish the Reconstruction Finance Corporation with a $500 million fund to provide emergency loans to banks and large industries in financial trouble.

But the prohibition issue, more than anything else, put a period to Texas Guinan's way of living.

The Wickersham Commission's report of January 19 concluded that the country was no longer able to enforce the Volstead Act, because of the high profits in the liquor trade and public antipathy— even outright hostility — to the law, and recommended that the act be modified as a function of the federal government alone rather than a joint federal-state undertaking. The Massachusetts legislature went further, calling upon Congress to start proceedings for a constitutional convention to consider repeal of the Eighteenth Amendment.

Texas looked for a new outlet. Her manager, John Stein, contracted with Harry Pilcer, famed French dancer and night club representative, for a summer engagement at Montmartre, the famous artist and cafe center in the northern part of Paris. Pilcer also owned a club which had closed, and in which Texas might wish to invest her money. There was a suggestion that en route to France, she might stop briefly with her troupe in London.

Guinan closed her show at the Argonaut the last week in May. "I plan to take my girls on a tour of Europe," she told her patrons, and with manager Stein, thirty "really ravishing blondes," along with a jazz band, boarded the French liner *Paris*.

Texas recalled: "We had a wonderful trip on the steamer — a whale of a time all the way." Many of the passengers from the *Paris*, however, expressed other convictions upon arriving at Plymouth, England. The troupe had entertained one evening at the ship's concert. Bedecked in a white riding habit and smart white boots, and spurred according to her ideal of the American cowgirl, Texas wisecracked about Lady Godiva and that she herself might "ride down the strand [seashore] on a white horse." Her girls appeared attired solely in garments made of two fans — one in front and the other in back. Several members of the clergy in the audience were "struck with dismay" when, during the entertainment, "some of the fans closed up."

Scotland Yard detectives notified Texas aboard the liner that she could not land in England. A complete dossier on her career had been assembled at Whitehall, and she was "on the government's list of barred aliens." Further, the unemployed of British variety and other artists were critical; the Ministry of Labor felt that admission of alien entertainers would make it more so.

Texas did not attempt to leave the *Paris*. "I will gladly give a check for a hundred thousand dollars to any charity if anyone can substantiate statements made against my character," she told reporters. "What has England against me? My parents were born in Great Britain."

She complimented at length the girls in her troupe. None of them drank, she said, and as for herself: "I've never had a drink and never sold a drink in my life."

Referring to her performance on the ship, she asked: "Is it because I said I would ride down the strand on a white horse? If you can find any statute in the laws of England which makes it criminal to ride a white horse I'll make you my heir."

Whitehall watered down its policy. Miss Guinan's application would be "referred to the Overseas Department of the Ministry, should the authorities at the Home Office see no objection to her visit."

Texas made no application, nor did her manager. "I don't care," she said. "I will come back someday, because England will want my company, as does every civilized country. We are not out to make money. We want to make people happy."

She cast longing eyes at the British shore as the liner proceeded to Havre, France.

Arriving at Havre, May 29, she found the French government even more adamant. Special police boarded the ship, and after examining passports, declared that the "Guinan gang" must remain on the liner until it returned to New York; that "instead of obtaining the visas required of entertainers who intended to exercise their profession in France," the "gang" had come "equipped only with tourist authorization." For this reason, the French Ministry of Labor forbade their fulfilling the Pilcer contract to perform at Montmartre.

The Paris press seemed more realistic: "The French Syndicate of Entertainers has been protesting to Premier [Pierre] Laval against the employment of foreigners, and . . . this circumstance may have actuated the special decree."

Texas echoed the report: "I have been turned back at the frontier for reasons which are vague, even in the minds of Frenchmen." Then she strongly declared: "I am an American citizen, and I have never been convicted of a crime. There is no scandal about me, and my passport is O.K.!"

In late afternoon, she told reporters: "The people do not understand my Broadway idiom at all, and ask some of the most astounding questions. When I referred to my girls as 'my kids,' some unknowing French dairymen interpreted it to mean that I was bringing a lot of sheep to confuse their trade system . . .''

In her baggage one assiduous customs agent discovered a set of fierce-looking bowie knives, which Texas, safely enough, threw against a corkboard while one of her "kids" stood nonchalantly in front of it. When the agent asked what she did with the knives, she replied, "I throw them at my girls." She later described his reaction: "He exclaimed and threw up his hands in a gesture which showed plainly that such a dangerous person would be no asset to France." Texas received the same reaction to a matched pair of six-shooters she used with the show.

Harry Pilcer gained one concession from the officials: Texas and her girls were brought ashore to spend the night at the Hotel Transatlantique, a "bunkhouse" affair which the French Line maintained for third-class emigrants. The girls were far from thrilled with their "unostentatious" quarters. Pilcer tried to console them and departed for Paris "to intervene with authorities."

The troupe's plight captured the conversation in night spots of Havre. One cable dispatch said: "From Tortoni's, with its elongated bar, to the humbler establishments on the waterfront, frequented by sailors and longshoremen, the talk is of 'Texas.' "

While some predicted that the ban would be lifted and the "Guinan gang" would come to Paris with an "extra blaze of publicity," Clement Vautel, columnist for the Paris *Le Journal*, noted that France was the "original home of night clubs and gayety and didn't need lessons from America." He added that the French could manage their own "whoopee," and urged that Miss Guinan "had much better stay home in this season of unemployment." A spokesman at the American Embassy was quoted as saying: "Nothing can be done in Miss Guinan's behalf . . . she will have to comply with the French laws."

Pilcer's efforts at the French capital were "ineffectual." The French Entertainers and Musicians Association and "numerous other habitual performers" in Montmartre petitioned the government to keep Texas from invading their territory "when the French are lacking work."

The edict from the French minister of labor was delivered to the night club queen at the Havre Hotel on the afternoon of May

30. The government had no objections to the "Guinan methods" and "regretted" that she had not asked for a permit before she set out for France, but it could not "grant her leave to remain." She must be on the *Paris* when the liner lifted anchor at 2:00 P.M., on June 3.

Manager Stein appealed to the French minister of the interior to review the decision, and Texas asked permission to go to Paris alone to plead her case with Premier Laval. "I have not come to France to occupy a salaried position, but to open a club in which I intend to invest my own money," she said. "France was only too glad to welcome me when I worked for her during the war . . . I appeal to the well known chivalry and courtesy of France to give me a chance to carry out my purpose."

Some excitement was caused during the night by reports that several young girls had been seen riding in automobiles in Paris, and later, in Montmartre establishments. One young woman who sang and danced at the Colonial Exposition restaurant and then disappeared was rumored to be a truant from the Guinan entourage.

Texas denied the reports by telephone. "My kids are all with me," she said, at the Hotel Transatlantique. "They have not budged and there isn't any big attraction keeping them here either."

Next day, author Channing Pollock telephoned to offer her the use of his house when she came to Paris. "He asked when I would come," she told reporters. "I said I would draw a couple of more cards first. I am not licked. There are lots of strings in my bow."

Other calls and telegrams poured in. One American steamship company offered to employ her aboard a liner on a world tour. And the owner of one of Monte Carlo's best-known clubs wired assurance that he had obtained official approval for her to come to Monaco to "furnish night-life joy this Summer," which also would enable her to make frequent trips into France since there was no border control between Monaco and the French Riviera.

A most startling offer came from a young Londoner, Harry Aslett, who arrived at Havre asking to marry her. He had no money, he said, but for five pounds she could enter England as his wife and then divorce him. "I'm sorry I can't marry you," she told Aslett. "I have too many expenses already."

No word came from the minister of the interior or Premier

Laval. Texas remained hopeful. "I don't mind for myself, but I do so want my kids to have the broadening influence of foreign travel. They're the prettiest kids in the world and with just a little culture they'd be knockouts." And the members of her party, though dining that night in depressed spirits, chorused: "We'll bet on Tex. She'll get us there yet!"

The detention began to take its toll, however. Texas remembered Sunday, May 31, as "the most miserable day in our lives. With the French Secret Service guarding the hotel doors, we simply stayed in bed."

Two of her "kids" bestirred themselves early and asked a watchful agent for permission to attend mass at a nearby church. The agent shrugged his shoulders. If the decision rested with him, he explained, the situation might be different, but his instructions were "rigid." No member of the party was to leave the Transatlantique.

It was a "greatly subdued" group that the gong summoned to luncheon in the third-class dining room. "I could stand it if those bells were not forever clanging," one girl wailed. Another, Anne Boleyn, became hysterical and ran from the hotel when a reporter attempted to interview her. The police brought her back. Some of the other girls then burst into tears, crying: "We'll never get to Paris! Let's go home!"

"I don't care where we go so long as we go some place," another dancer moaned.

Texas spent the afternoon in her cramped quarters, with three narrow beds and barred windows. "She is worn out and has a splitting headache," Bunny Weldon, director of the chorus, told visitors. "She can't see anybody."

The Paris newspaper *Oeuvre* of June 1, somewhat mystified by the government's strong measures, printed a photograph of "Guinan's Broadway Belles" with the query: "WHAT? THESE UNDESIRABLES? WE SHOULD LIKE TO SEE SOME THAT WE WOULD WANT, THEN."

Columnist P. J. Philip wrote: "France, like every other nation, is a protectionist country, not only in matters of commerce but in matters of labor . . . There probably are fewer restrictions here than anywhere, yet even here the public is tiring of being made to cross the street only where the police permit."

Public bewilderment to the contrary, Director Mourier of the Surete Generals police at the Ministry of the Interior reiterated the government's edict. The pleas of Miss Guinan, her manager, and friends had failed to alter the minister of labor's decision.

Upon receiving the message at Havre, Texas remarked: "Well, in the words of [ex-President Calvin] Coolidge, 'I do not choose to run.' " This fruitless visit to the shores of Europe had cost her "fifty grand," and she said she might not be able to pay for the return passage. "I have nothing more to say," was her final word.

The question was settled the evening of June 2, when a representative of the French Lines reported that his company had agreed to take the party back to New York without charge, in first-class accommodations. It was intimated that the decision had been reached at the request of Premier Laval, and that the French government might stand part of the expense.

The party spent the night making ready for their departure, while additional detectives posted at the hotel prevented any "escapes" and demanded credentials of all who entered or left.

"I was a sucker to come 3,000 miles to go to jail when every jail in America is waiting for me," Texas quipped to the press. "But you know — an indiscretion a day keeps depression away."

As she and her girls were courteously but firmly assisted up the gangplank of the *Paris* the following afternoon, they paused repeatedly to pose for photographers. "It all goes to show," Texas shouted, "that fifty million French can be wrong. I should have seen Premier Laval."

The "gang" lined the rail and waved farewell as the steamer slipped out to sea. Police agents waited on the dock until the ship disappeared in the late afternoon mist. It left behind Harry Aslett, who sat forlornly on his suitcase at the pier, bemoaning his fate and unable to accompany the party to Plymouth because of the lack of funds.

Texas cloistered her girls on the return journey to America. She declined to entertain at the ship's concert, and the disappointed crew complained to Capt. Luc de Maigiaive: "We might as well be bringing back a crowd of diplomats."

The liner docked at New York's West Fifteenth Street pier June 9. Standing in her cabin, with "practically a thousand cablegrams and radiograms in her hands," Texas met reporters and friends who had crowded on the boarding cutter *Wissachickon* to be among the first to greet her.

"She was in good form," said the *Times,* "with 'Do you get

what I mean?' and 'Just listen to this' interspersed in her rapidfire description of those melancholy five days spent in a detention hotel at Havre." Passport laws aside, she credited the bar to her entry to nervous club and restaurant owners who felt that she "would undoubtedly take away all their night-life trade." She considered this a compliment, which "served in certain degree to mitigate the bitterness she and her girls had experienced at France's receptiveness."

It also became the basis for a satirical revue, with herself in the cast, appropriately titled *Too Hot for Paris*.

CHAPTER 12

Broadway Thru A Keyhole

Too Hot for Paris, of varied authorship, took the form of a night club show, including popular performers Jack Osterman, Joe Frisco, the Neal Sisters and Dick Lane, a fourteen-piece band, and ten ravishing blondes in addition to the thirty that had accompanied Texas Guinan to France. It opened at Bayes Theater, which recently had housed Al Jolson's starring vehicle *The Wonder Bar* (also employing a night club background), and played "at a $3 top."

During August, Texas and her company appeared at the Woodsmansten Inn, Pelham, New York.

Within weeks, she had recuperated most of her losses. *Too Hot for Paris* was such a success that she decided to begin a one-year transcontinental tour in the company's own buses. This venture was sponsored by the Orchestra Corporation of America, which shortly announced that it had booked 200 one- and two-night stands in cities and towns across the country.

"The show can be set up on a prairie if need be," Texas said. "We even carry our own applause."

With forty-six performers, her musicians and drivers, "Miss Guinan took leave of New York" Saturday afternoon, September 19. A crowd of several hundred gathered around the motor caravan at Forty-ninth Street and Broadway, while she posed for newsreel cameras and wisecracked her farewell "so's the city can get a good, long sleep."

She predicted that the country would have light wines and beer by New Year's Day and that "prosperity would return with this refreshment." (Her reference was to the pending Beer-Wine Revenue Bill which Congress eventually approved March 22, 1933, amending the Volstead Act to legalize wine, beer, lager beer, ale, and "porter's beer" of 3.2% maximum alcoholic content, and levying a tax of $5 per barrel aimed at securing additional funds for the U.S. treasury.) She also touched on such varied subjects as night club girls and habitués, evangelist Aimee McPherson, and Mayor Jimmy Walker. (Mayor Walker would resign several months later after a lengthy investigation into myriad charges of graft and corruption in his administration.)

As for evangelist McPherson, Texas alluded to Nancy Barr Mavity's *Sister Aimee,* a biography just published by Doubleday, Doran and Company, in which the author called Miss McPherson "astoundingly egotistic" and "the Barnum of religion" but defended her against charges of scandal and hypocrisy. "Someday I would like to debate Miss McPherson," Texas said. "If you compare the lives of the evangelist and myself since we were little girls, you will find they have run parallel in many respects. She, too, is a mighty clever woman."

Finally, Texas proclaimed: "This trip is an anti-depression tour . . . My company will donate a portion of its earnings in each city to local unemployment relief."

From Bridgeport, Connecticut, where the revue played that night, the company intended to cover New England, then start westward. However, in several New England towns the show was banned when "its nature was learned."

At the clock manufacturing city of Waltham, Massachusetts, the show was canceled by the "express order" of Mayor Patrick J. Duane, who declared: "If the show's too hot for Paris, it's too hot for Waltham."

Texas carried her battle to the mayor's office after he declined to discuss the matter by phone. Though she argued, cajoled, and pleaded with his honor for half an hour, her only satisfaction was the sympathy of most of the populace.

"Some people are so narrow-minded that their ears touch in back," she quipped to 10,000 persons who milled about the auditorium where the performance was to be held. "The mayor of this watch city has given me the works."

The situation improved considerably as the show moved into Pennsylvania, with "three-night engagements" at Wilkes-Barre and other cities. In repeated performances of her Wild West act in Chicago, Texas recalled: "I got shooting pains."

She also received the manuscript of a play titled *All Wet,* written by Dr. Ralph Culver Bennett, a former assistant state's attorney in Chicago, then dean of the Law School of the University of Oregon and a lecturer on motion picture law at the University of Southern California. *All Wet,* a farce based on the Mavity book *Sister Aimee,* depicted the three stages of Miss McPherson's life.

Bennett was at the Bristol Hotel in New York. Charles Hopkins would direct the play on Broadway. Helen Rowland, the child actress, would have the role of Miss McPherson as a child, and Edith Barrett would personate the evangelist as a girl. The question was, would Miss Guinan bring the characterization to date?

Texas read part of the manuscript and was receptive. Bennett wired to bring the script to New York, that Hopkins wished to begin preparation of the dramatization immediately.

The *Times* of January 14, 1932, reported: "Texas Guinan arrived from Chicago yesterday afternoon . . . in an ensemble of flaming red flannel trimmed with leopard skin and with a jewelled lorgnette hanging from her neck — a costume apparently befitting one whose 'life has run parallel,' as she expressed it, to that of Miss McPherson . . . William Egan, station master of the Pennsylvania, several porters and a large group of track walkers who were present seemed slightly bewildered when Miss Guinan greeted her mother and father, a quiet, gray-haired couple, with 'Hello, kids.' " At her flat at 17 West Eighth Street, "Miss Guinan said that she had come to produce a play based on Nancy Mavity's *Sister Aimee.*"

The manuscript? She had given it to her theatrical manager, John Stein, to read, and told Bennett at the Bristol Hotel that, in the hustle and bustle of scheduling *Too Hot for Paris,* Stein had misplaced it. Stein admitted that the script had been lost.

The angered Bennett did not believe them. It was his only copy of the play. On February 24 he named Texas and John Stein defendants in a summons charging them with unlawfully withholding *All Wet.*

He was unable to serve the summons for Miss Guinan at her

17 West Eighth Street address. She had rejoined Stein and her show in Chicago. On March 2, Magistrate Van Amringe of the West Side Court dismissed the case and told Bennett his only recourse was civil action.

Meanwhile, Doubleday, Doran and Company declared they had equal dramatic rights with the author to the book and those rights had not been sold — something that Bennett as an authority on motion picture law should have known. He dropped his suit.

At almost every stand, Texas joked about having been turned back at the French frontier and asked her cheering audiences to imagine why her show had been rejected for Parisian consumption. The attendant publicity apparently proved embarrassing to the French.

Texas recalled what happened: "You can imagine my surprise when a letter came from the secretary to the President of France, inviting me to visit their dear old Paris as a guest of the government . . . They wished to show me that Paris and Frenchmen were not such a hard lot and could appreciate the better things of life after all."

Texas wished to "buy many costumes" for her summer tour. Where else except Paris could she find "the unusual"? She accepted the invitation. She arrived in Paris on May 10, stayed ten days, and returned to New York on the North German Lloyd liner *Europa,* May 27.

"I learned to love France when I was there with the American Army," she told *Times* reporters, adding that the country had "received and entertained her so well" she was "almost speechless."

"There is such a difference between the United States and France — people here do not know how to live," she said, and thought she might "make her home there" within a couple of years.

No longer avengeful, she retitled her show *The Texas Guinan Revue,* and once more traveled the circuits of her younger days. Florida, where she had made her "first bundle" in the real estate boom, and New Orleans were on her itinerary.

She had planned a side trip to Havana, but came back to New York in the fall in favor of a vaudeville engagement at Rochester. She flew to Buffalo on October 12 to fill a special club appearance and returned to Rochester, October 13, where she disclosed that Mortimer Davis, Jr., a Montreal theater manager, was her husband-to-be in a fourth matrimonial venture.

The Associated Press reported that Mortimer Davis, Jr., had married Roszika Dolly, one of the Dancing Dolly Sisters, at Brewster, New York, in March 1927, and divorced her at Mineola in February 1932. He was the son of the late Sir Mortimer Davis, Canadian capitalist.

"He is the only man in the world who can make me laugh," Texas said. "We will be married Christmas day at Sherbrooke, Quebec, Canada."

She failed to explain later why the wedding never took place.

Nor did she comment on the demise of her early mentor, Larry Fay. Fay's last night club in New York City was the Casa Blanca. As bad times began to pinch, he cut the salaries of his employees drastically. An easily aroused doorman shot him to death in his establishment, January 2, 1933.

Texas talked of reentering the night club business, but the repeal of prohibition was imminent. By November 1932, President Hoover's name had become anathema to millions of Americans, and Democrat Franklin D. Roosevelt swept the hapless president out of office by a plurality larger than that by which Hoover had defeated Alfred E. Smith. Congress also became heavily Democratic. On February 20, 1933, as the nation careened dizzily with the hope that Roosevelt would somehow bring a return to prosperity, Congress adopted a resolution to repeal the Eighteenth Amendment. As a proposed Twenty-first Amendment, it went to the states for ratification.

Assisted by brother Tommy and her advance man, Eddie Baker, Texas again toured the western circuits, this time as far as San Francisco. Her entourage now included her favorite horse, Pieface, and she put more emphasis on her Wild West acts. In September, waving her sombrero and six-shooter, as frolicsome as ever, she rode Pieface down the streets of Pasadena in a Labor Day parade, alongside western movie greats Tom Mix, Buck Jones and others, and performed at "The Oklahoma Stampede," staged at the Rose Bowl to benefit the Mt. Sinai Home for Invalids.

At the same time, she contracted for a role in Darryl F. Zanuck's 20th Century production, *Broadway Thru A Keyhole,* in which a much-feared gangster, Frank Rocci (Paul Kelly), and a crooner, Clark Brian (Russ Columbo), vie for the affections of a virtuous girl, Joan Whelan (Constance Cummings).

The background was a New York night club operated by

Rocci, where theater-goers saw Sybil Smith (Blossom Seely), Texas Guinan (Tex Kaley), Eddie Foy, Jr., Abe Lyman and his band, and others, and were treated to several well-staged numbers such as "When You Were the Girl on the Scooter," "You're My Past, Present and Future," and "Doing the Uptown Lowdown."

The plot: Rocci meets Joan Whelan, decides she is to be his featured performer, and lives with the hope of making her his bride, while he battles his foes. The stage manager of the club, Max Mefooski (Gregory Ratoff), hesitates to disagree with Rocci, knowing that crossing the gangster virtually means committing suicide. As the plot thickens, Rocci thinks the bullets may fly and that his racketeer opponent, Tim Crowley (C. Henry Gordon), may try to even the odds by harming Joan. Rocci sends the girl, accompanied by Sybil Smith, to Florida. Here Joan encounters crooner Clark Brian. They fall in love. The fire flies between Brian and the notorious Rocci, who has Joan returned to New York by the first plane. Love turns Brian, who heretofore detests the sight of blood, into an individual willing to fight Rocci to a rattling finish.

The author of the story was the popular syndicated gossip columnist and radio commentator of the 1930s, Walter Winchell.

CHAPTER 13

Finale

Broadway Thru A Keyhole opened at the Rivoli, in New York, the week of November 1, 1933. Texas, however, was unavailable for the occasion. She and her forty fan-dancers had gone up the West Coast to the Pacific Northwest.

The tour was a strenuous one. In Oregon, she suffered intestinal pains, which continued in varying degree. She left brother Tommy to settle the show's affairs in Portland, telling him her illness was nothing serious.

She took her girls to Vancouver, British Columbia, and on the night of October 30, performed before an audience of thousands. After the show, in severe pain, she was rushed to the Vancouver General Hospital. Dr. A. J. MacLachlan diagnosed her illness as amoebic dysentery.

Her condition seemed satisfactory until the morning of November 4, when a sudden relapse caused by perforation of the bowel necessitated an immediate operation. Texas went into the operating room in a cheerful mood, but confided to Dr. Mac-Lachlan that she was willing to die if it would relieve her suffering. That night, surgeons announced that death was only a matter of hours.

She received the last rites and communion from the Reverend

Father Louis Forget of St. Patrick's Church. Her forty girls were grief-stricken. Texas repeated to Dr. MacLachlan the assertion she had made in local and federal courts many times: "I've never touched alcohol in my life." She asked her advance man, Eddie Baker, to return her body to Broadway: "I'd rather have a square inch of New York than all the rest of the world." She died at 8:00 the next morning, November 5, 1933, at the age of forty-nine.

Tommy Guinan arrived too late. Fog had forced cancellation of his passage on a northbound plane. He left Portland by bus to Seattle and proceeded to Vancouver by boat.

Tommy and the show troupe accompanied the body on the train to Chicago, where they transferred to the Pennsylvania Manhattan Limited, and reached New York on November 11. The body was taken to the Campbell Funeral Church on Broadway between Sixty-sixth and Sixty-seventh streets, where it would lie in state Sunday, November 12, pending services.

During the afternoon, nearly 12,000 persons entered the church through the Broadway door, passed in single file up three short flights of stairs to the second floor, through the family reception room massed with flowers strewn over and about its gilded French furniture, and exited through the Sixty-seventh Street door. Newsreel cameramen filmed the throng passing the bier.

"Miss Guinan's body was dressed in a white chiffon sequin gown — she had been partial to sequins," said the *Times*. "In her left hand was a rosary and upon the third finger a large diamond. Another diamond of comparable size was upon the little finger of her right hand. Around her neck was a diamond pendant. Part of the silver-colored bronze coffin was covered with orchids . . .

"The file was never still, and mostly dry-eyed. It was like a Broadway crowd thinned out so that every passing face was distinct. Women whose clothes showed they came from homes of culture stood in line with others in tawdry raiment."

A few celebrities viewed the body, among them Jacob Ruppert, owner of the New York Yankees, and the stage and radio entertainer Jack Pearl. Pearl paused to say: "She was the most lovable and honorable girl Broadway has ever known."

Police Inspector John O'Brien assigned fifty patrolmen and two sergeants to guard the crowd of some 7,500 that gathered for the funeral at 2:00 P.M. on Monday. The throng packed Broadway for a block and overflowed into the center parkway. Admittance to the chapel was by card only.

In the front pew sat the Guinan family. Also in the first pews were the honorary pallbearers and pallbearers, among whom were stage-door columnists Heywood Broun, Mark Hellinger, Edward Sullivan, O. O. McIntyre, and Louis Sobol; the orchestra leader Paul Whiteman; and attorneys Maxwell Lopin and Walter B. Sollinger.

The Reverend J. McKenna of St. Malachy's Roman Catholic Church read a prayer for the dead in Latin, which was followed by brief eulogies by Heywood Broun and Lambert Fairchild, chaplain of the Captain Belvidere Brooks Post of the American Legion (made up almost entirely of vaudeville entertainers). Visibly upset and eyes wet, Broun reminded those "who loved Texas very much" that she would be "kept in the hearts and minds of those who knew her." Chaplain Fairchild spoke of her service as an entertainer in France during the war.

Before the casket was closed, the two large diamonds on her fingers and the diamond pendant around her neck were removed by members of the family.

At 3:00 P.M. the body was taken to White Plains, New York, for burial in a vault in the Gate of Heaven Cemetery. More than 500 cars joined the cortege. The White Plains police estimated it to be the longest funeral procession the city had ever witnessed.

The exuberant Broadway hostess had made hundreds of thousands of dollars out of her troubles. Where the money went, nobody knew. Her will, filed November 24, named her mother sole heir to her estate. Its value was not disclosed. Attorney Sollinger was the executor.

Her personal property was moved to the auction rooms of Benjamin Marx at 24 West Fifty-eighth Street and sold on December 19–20 to "professional dealers, a multitude of the curious and a sprinkling of celebrities," who "chortled" when they got such bargains as jeweled cigarette boxes for fifty and seventy-five cents and garish floor lamps for a dollar.

A black and green enameled vanity case set with diamonds and inscribed "Listen, Miss Tex. E." — given to her by the Prince of Wales — was knocked down after lively bidding for $125. A boudoir doll sold for $4.25, and a carved teakwood screen given her by the serial queen Pearl White went for $13. An elaborate, nine-carat

diamond ring given to her by the late President Warren G. Harding
for her work in his campaign of 1920 was purchased by a dealer for
$1,525. A pearl and diamond bracelet, the gift of the late actor,
playwright, and theatrical producer David Belasco, sold for $155.
And a "prize piece" — a diamond bracelet with an assortment of
large stones and 586 small ones — went to a dealer for $1,875. Her
gowns and other apparel were given to friends.

On the concluding day of the sale, a bullet-proof auto Texas
had bought from the late Larry Fay at first found no bidders, then
finally was knocked down to a car dealer for $80. Her personal au-
tomobile was bought for $400 by a Pennsylvania antracite mine
owner for his daughter.

Other assorted items ranged from a synagogue chair "whose
history no one knows," to a gold-plated, sterling silver, coral-inlaid
telephone; a gold-encrusted dinner service of more than 100 pieces
with platinum medallions, which Texas never used; tables, chairs,
and other pieces of furniture; a reducing machine; a vacuum
cleaner "filled with dust"; and several rare books, including autographed presentation copies of Thornton Wilder's *Bridge of San Luis
Rey,* the German edition of Sinclair Lewis's *Dodsworth,* Nan Brit-
ton's *The President's Daughter,* and Carl Van Vechten's *Peter Whiffle.*

Attorney Sollinger bought Miss Guinan's signed photograph
and "coat of arms," with the motto "Have you a little padlock on
your home?"

The two-day session, according to the *Times,* netted some
$12,500.

Two years later, Miss Guinan's remains were transferred to
the family plot in Calvary Cemetery, Queens.

On December 5, 1933 — a month from the day of her death at
Vancouver — the Eighteenth Amendment was repealed as Utah
became the thirty-sixth state to ratify the Twenty-first Amendment
to the Constitution.

Prohibition made Texas Guinan famous. It is fitting that they
went out together.

Afterword:
The Impersonators

For decades, beginning two months before Texas Guinan's death, several actresses have impersonated her on both the stage and screen.

In September 1933, Columbia Pictures released *Lady For A Day*, based on Damon Runyon's merry, sentimental tale "Madam La Gimp," in which gangsters help Apple Annie, a fruit peddler (played by May Robson), to pose as the rich, gray-haired Mrs. E. Worthington Manville (not for just a day, but for a week) when she learns that her daughter Louise (Jean Parker) is on her way to New York with a young Spanish nobleman (Walter Connolly), to whom she is engaged. Dave the Dude (Warren William) and his band of ruffians live in a style suited to the Manville name. Guy Kibbe wins laurels carrying off the part of Judge Blake, one of Dave's elder underlings. Glenda Farrell splits the posies and looks great in her Guinan role as Missouri Martin, New York's famed night club hostess.

Incendiary Blonde, a lavish technicolor production of Paramount Pictures in 1945, cast Betty Hutton as Texas Guinan, Barry Fitzgerald as Michael Guinan, and Mary Phillips as Bessie Guinan, with Arturo de Cordova, Charlie Ruggles, and Albert Dekker in the roles of Bill Kilgannon, Cherokee Jim, and Caddo, respectively.

119

The story begins with a fast-paced rodeo in which Texas busts a bronc for a $50 prize and becomes the star of the show, then goes on to become a chorus girl, a featured entertainer on Broadway, and heroine of two-reel silent films. The balance of the picture is devoted to a laundered conception of her life during the cabaret-crazy Prohibition twenties. Intended to be biographical, *Incendiary Blonde* takes many liberties with Texas Guinan's real life. Of course, the producer was trying to please the thousands of moviegoers of the 1940s who had only a slight familiarity with the entertainer's name or personality, and in this Paramount was successful.

In *Splendor in the Grass,* a Warner Brothers release of October 1961 starring Natalie Wood and Warren Beatty, Texas Guinan is impersonated briefly by none other than Phyllis Diller. *Splendor* is the haunting story of adolescent love and adult passion which begins in a small Kansas town during the late 1920s and runs the gamut of the stock market crash and the Great Depression. The location scenes were filmed at Staten Island and High Falls, New York. The source of the film title is Wordsworth's "Ode on Intimations of Immortality."

In November 1961, little more than a month after the release of *Splendor in the Grass, The George Raft Story* opened in Chicago. This 105-minute Allied Artists bio-drama starred George Raft, Jayne Mansfield, and Julie London, supported by more than a dozen other well-known actors and actresses including Barbara Nichols as Texas Guinan. The production is replete with bootleggers, gangsters, dancers, cigarette girls, gamblers, hotels, casinos, night clubs, New York City, Hell's Kitchen, and dabbles with the careers of Al Capone and Benny "Bugsy" Siegel.

The songstress, Jane Morgan, announced in March 1968 that she would star in a Broadway musical based on the life of Texas Guinan. It never materialized.

Comedienne Martha Raye had little success with her musical stage version of the Texas Guinan story in 1969. The show, aptly titled "Hello, Sucker!," tried out in Connecticut but never made it to Broadway.

If the *real* story of this wisecracking and defiant first lady of Prohibition-era night clubs is brought to the screen, it should be, in the words of one Guinan biographer, "a humdinger!"

Bibliography

Newspapers

Chicago Daily Tribune. January 1906.
New York Times. January 1906; August 1925; February–April, July, September–October, December 1927; April–October, 1928; April, June–July, October, 1929; March, May, October–December, 1930; May–June, August–September, 1931; January–March, May, October, 1932; January, May–June, November–December, 1933.

Periodicals

Exhibitors Herald & Moving Picture World (combined issue), Vol. 92, no. 8/ vol. 34, no. 11 (August 25, 1928).
Motion Picture Magazine. Vol. 11, no. 1 (February 1916) through vol. 12, no. 8 (September 1916); vol. 15, no. 1 (February 1918). M.P. Publishing Company, Brooklyn, New York.
Moving Picture World. Vol. 24, no. 12 (June 19, 1915) through vol. 26, no. 10 (November 27, 1915); vol. 27, no. 8 (February 26, 1916) through vol. 29, no. 9 (August 26, 1916); vol. 31, no. 10 (March 10, 1917) through vol. 34, no. 11 (December 17, 1917); vol. 35, no. 5 (August 3, 1918) through vol. 37, no. 9 (August 31, 1918); vol. 40, no. 6 (May 10, 1919) through vol. 42, no. 8 (December 20, 1919); vol. 43, no. 2 (January 10, 1920) through vol. 46, no. 7 (October 16, 1920); vol. 48, no. 7 (February 12, 1921) through vol. 52, no. 1 (September 3, 1921). Chalmers Publishing Company, New York.
Photoplay Magazine. Vol. 9, no. 3 (February 1916); vol. 11, no. 3 (February 1917). Photoplay Publishing Company, Chicago, Illinois.
Picture-Play Magazine. Vol. 5, no. 5 (January 1917); vol. 8, no. 5 (July 1918); vol. 10, no. 1 (March 1919). Street and Smith, New York.
This Was Show Business. (annual). Literary Enterprises, Inc., New York, 1956.

Books

American Heritage History of the 20's & 30's. New York: The American Heritage Publishing Company, Inc., 1970.

Beach, Frederick Converse (editor-in-chief). *The Americana*. 16 vols. New York: Scientific American Compiling Department, 1903–1906.

Blum, Daniel. *A Pictorial History of the Talkies*. New York: Grossett & Dunlap, Publishers, 1958.

———. *A Pictorial History of the Silent Screen*. New York: G. P. Putnam's Sons, 1953.

Botkin, B. A. (editor). *New York City Folklore*. New York: Random House, 1956.

Brown, Henry Collins. *New York of Today*. New York: The Old Colony Press, 1917.

Brownlow, Kevin. *The War, the West and the Wilderness*. New York: Alfred A. Knopf, 1979.

Eames, John Douglas. *The Paramount Story*. New York: Crown Publishers, Inc., 1985.

Ewen, David. *The Complete Book of the American Musical Theater*. New York, Chicago and San Francisco: Holt, Rinehart and Winston, 1970.

The Fabulous Century 1900–1910. New York: Time-Life Books, 1970.

——— *1910–1920*. New York: Time-Life Books, 1970.

——— *1920–1930*. New York: Time-Life Books, 1970.

Fell, John. *A History of Films*. New York, Chicago, San Francisco, Atlanta, Montreal, Toronto: Holt, Rinehart and Winston, 1979.

Film Year Book 1922–1923. New York and Hollywood: Wid's Films & Film Folks, Inc.

——— *1924*. New York and Hollywood: Publishers of the Film Daily.

——— *1925*. New York and Hollywood: Publishers of the Film Daily.

Green, Abel, and Joe Laurie, Jr. *Show Biz from Vaude to Video*. New York: Henry Holt and Company, 1951.

Halliwell, Leslie. *Mountain of Dreams. The Golden Years of Paramount Pictures*. New York: Stonehill Publishing Company, 1976.

Horan, James D. *The Desperate Years. A Pictorial History of the Thirties. From Stock Market Crash to World War II*. New York: Bonanza Books, 1962.

James, Edward T. (editor). *Notable American Women, 1607–1950*. 2 vols. Cambridge: Belknap Press of Harvard University, 1971.

Koszarski, Diane Kaiser. *The Complete Films of William S. Hart. A Pictorial Record*. New York: Dover Publications, Inc., 1980.

Krafsur, Richard P. (executive editor). *The American Film Institute Catalog of Motion Pictures. Feature Films 1961–1970*. 2 vols. New York and London: R. R. Bowker Company, 1976.

Lahue, Kalton C. *Continued Next Week. A History of the Moving Picture Serial*. Norman: University of Oklahoma Press, 1964.

————. *Winners of the West. The Sagebrush Heroes of the Silent Screen.* South Brunswick and New York: A. S. Barnes and Company, Thomas Yoseloff, Ltd., London, 1970.

Laurie, Joe, Jr. *Vaudeville from the Honky-Tonks to the Palace.* New York: Henry Holt and Company, 1953.

Lauritzen, Einar, and Gunnar Lundquist. *American Film-Index 1908–1915.* Stockholm, Sweden: Film-Index, 1976.

Mix, Paul E. *The Life and Legend of Tom Mix.* South Brunswick and New York: A. S. Barnes and Company, Thomas Yoseloff, Ltd., London, 1972.

Motion Picture Studio Directory and Trade Annual 1921. Chicago, New York and Los Angeles: Motion Picture News, Inc.

Munden, Kenneth W. (executive editor). *The American Film Institute Catalog of Motion Pictures Produced in the United States. Feature Films 1921–1930.* 2 vols. New York and London: R. R. Bowker Company, 1971.

New York Times Film Reviews 1913–1968. 5 vols. New York: New York Times and Arno Press, 1970.

Nicholas, John H. *Tom Mix Riding Up to Glory.* A Persimmon Hill Book. Oklahoma City: National Cowboy Hall of Fame and Western Heritage Center, 1980.

Sann, Paul. *The Lawless Decade. A Pictorial History of A Great American Transition from the World War I Armistice and Prohibition to Repeal and the New Deal.* New York: Crown Publishers, Inc., 1957.

Sylvester, Robert. *No Cover Charge. A Backward Look at the Night Clubs.* New York: The Dial Press, 1956.

Taylor, Deems, Marcelene Peterson, and Bryant Hale. *A Pictorial History of the Movies.* New York: Simon and Schuster, 1930.

Variety Film Reviews 1907–1980. 16 vols. New York and London: Garland Publishing, Inc., 1983.

Weaver, John T. (compiler). *Twenty Years of Silents 1908–1928.* Metuchen, New Jersey: The Scarecrow Press, Inc., 1971.

Webb, Walter Prescott, and H. Bailey Carroll (editors). *The Handbook of Texas.* 2 vols. Austin: Texas State Historical Association, 1952.

Wid's Year Book 1920–1921. New York and Hollywood: Wid's Films & Film Folks, Inc.

———— *1921–1922.* New York and Hollywood: Wid's Films & Film Folks, Inc.

Articles

Bacon, James. "Before It Was Legal She Was Sexy." *Showcase (Daily Oklahoman)*, April 29, 1973.

Braun, Eric. "One For the Boys." *Films and Filming*, vol. 17, no. 2 (November 1970).

Buchman, Chris. "Mae West, 1892–1980." *Classic Images*, no. 73 (January 1981).

Fernett, Gene. "The Historic Film Studios (Triangle)." *Classic Images*, no. 110 (August 1984).

Robinson, David. "Hollywood in the Twenties." *Film Journal Advertiser*, vol. 1, no. 10 (June 1970).

Stumpf, Charles K. "Rootin', Tootin', Two-Gun Shootin', Texas Guinan." *Under Western Skies*, no. 9 (January 1980).

Tarbox, Charles. "Early Productions." *8MM Collector*, no. 3 (December 31, 1962).

Winn, Emery. "The Time I Saw Texas Guinan." *Oklahoma's Orbit (Daily Oklahoman)*, February 7, 1965.